The Thing about Florida

UNIVERSITY PRESS OF FLORIDA

Florida A&M University, Tallahassee
Florida Atlantic University, Boca Raton
Florida Gulf Coast University, Ft. Myers
Florida International University, Miami
Florida State University, Tallahassee
New College of Florida, Sarasota
University of Central Florida, Orlando
University of Florida, Gainesville
University of North Florida, Jacksonville
University of South Florida, Tampa
University of West Florida, Pensacola

The Thing

University Press of Florida

Gainesville · Tallahassee · Tampa · Boca Raton

Pensacola · Orlando · Miami · Jacksonville · Ft. Myers · Sarasota

☼ Tyler Gillespie

about Florida

Exploring a Misunderstood State

26   25   24   23   22   21   6   5   4   3   2   1

Library of Congress Control Number: 2020942567
ISBN: 978-0-8130-6687-5

The University Press of Florida is the scholarly publishing agency for the State
University System of Florida, comprising Florida A&M University, Florida Atlantic
University, Florida Gulf Coast University, Florida International University, Florida
State University, New College of Florida, University of Central Florida, University of
Florida, University of North Florida, University of South Florida, and University of
West Florida.

University Press of Florida
2046 NE Waldo Road
Suite 2100
Gainesville, FL 32609
http://upress.ufl.edu

Contents

BECAUSE FLORIDA

I dreaded childhood beach days with Mom because I burned in approximately 2.5 seconds. We lived in a small apartment next to a 24-hour carwash near the white-white sand of Florida's Clearwater Beach, often ranked as one of the best beaches in the United States. Mom woke up on weekdays around 4:00 a.m. to wait tables so she could help my grandparents pay for my tuition at a Christian school. I spent many nights with my Southern Baptist grandparents, but weekend beach days belonged to her and, begrudgingly, to me. I sometimes attempted to thwart her plans with my version of a rain dance. I lifted my hands and spastically moved my shoulders. These dances never seemed to work. Mom, a self-proclaimed beach bum, made us sandwiches and dragged me to her favorite place.

I've heard people say no one is born in Florida, but Mom and I were. I'm a fifth-generation Floridian. The maternal side of my family lived on the west coast for more than seventy years; before that, my family lived a few hours north in a town near Gainesville. I grew up in Largo, which I tell people is near Clearwater Beach, which is near St. Petersburg, which isn't far from Tampa, which is south of Orlando. People have thought I meant Key Largo, but Largo is about 330 miles north of the state's southernmost tip in Key West. Florida kind of looks like a gun, and some people I've known rock tattoos to prove it. My hometown in Pinellas County sits midway down the grip below the trigger. Retirees might know Pinellas as a mecca for the 55-and-over crowd. Fans of *Cops* might know it, too, as the area often appears on the TV show.

Most people, though, probably know this area best for its beaches. Mom had walked those beaches when the sand belonged to everyone. By the time we went together, rich people owned some of the beach's best parts. We never had the required access keys or code words or secret handshakes for this section of sand. Mom didn't care. We often went with Mom's friend who had two kids, and our group sneaked passed the guard's station to walk down the long, splintery boardwalk. We'd find a spot close but not too close to the water. Mom would lather on my sunscreen, smoke a Virginia Slims Menthol, and turn a radio's knob to her favorite station. She'd fall asleep for anywhere between ten minutes and two hours. I shuffled past stingrays to sandbars and perfected my hobby of picking up sand dollars between my toes. I remember days when pods of manatees swam by me along with dolphins and maybe once or twice a shark I thought was a dolphin. I built sandcastles on shore and sifted through coquinas. I could identify seashells: the tiger's eyes, conchs, and pyramids some people called cones.

Still, I hated the beach.

I hated the boiling-hot sand and the seagulls who liked to steal our potato chips. My list of beach-hates continued, but sunburns proved my main hate. They hurt and embarrassed me. They made me self-conscious, just as my native Florida status would start to do in my teenage years.

It's probably biological for teenagers to wish they had been born somewhere else. Their small town was too quiet or their place in the country was too country. For me, Florida became too "Florida." People could say almost anything about the state, and it would be true. Florida's been known as a sanitorium, a tourist destination, a retirement community. "The state is just everything at once," a comedian once said. "You'd never make Florida on purpose." My never-made-on-purpose state begat weird news stories, and those stories eventually begat the popular "because Florida" joke.

Because Florida, a grandmother was assaulted for a Facebook friend request snub. Because Florida, a woman "Fights to Keep Her Pet Alligator Who Wears Clothes and 'Rides' ATVs." Because Florida, there was a "Snake Farm Shooting."

The first "because Florida" punch line I remember came in the wake of the 2000 Gore versus Bush presidential election. The headlines about the inept recount made Floridians sound like toddlers who couldn't count. The term "chad" morphed into a four-letter word.

Deborah Clark had worked at the county's election's office since 1978 and was 2000's Pinellas supervisor of elections. Clark could have never imagined the scrutiny brought on by the recount. "That was an interesting five weeks after the election," said Clark. Florida's an important presidential swing state with a bunch of electoral college votes. It's bruised-fruit purple: voted red, then blue, then back to red. This 2000 election had been tight, and the public paid more attention to Clark's office than it ever had.

Clark's county encompassed my hometown and had used the same voting system for twenty-four years. The voting system had been solid, and it verified the unofficial results. Clark spent most of the 2000 postelection frenzy at the election service center. The big issue centered on the fact that Florida hadn't determined a legal definition of a valid vote. Clark found herself surrounded by big-bucks attorneys other states had seemingly airdropped. Staff members at the courthouse office sent Clark and her team flowers.

Voters had punched ballot cards, creating a little hole in the ballot by removing a piece of paper called a "chad." No one knew how much of the chad needed to be removed from the ballot to constitute a valid vote. One corner? Two corners? Three? "It sounds obvious now," said Clark. "Most things are clear in the rearview mirror." Palm Beach County faced the harshest criticism. They used a ballot nicknamed the "butterfly ballot" because pages faced each other like wings. Their supervisor of elections received death threats. She had to have a police escort. Florida and other states had used this type of layout for years without much negative feedback from voters. The recount changed the narrative. "In my opinion, people convinced voters they were confused by the ballot, and maybe some of them legitimately were," said Clark, "but we have to remind ourselves the media is a business, and they're looking for a story."

Election reform ultimately came out of the debacle. In 2001, the state senate passed an election reform bill that finally included a definition of a valid vote. But we got ahead of ourselves. A lot of the reform got repealed, and, unfortunately, Florida faced another big recount issue in 2018. A thin margin decided the gubernatorial race.

A national publication labeled us as the "Land of Recounts and Contested Elections." This headline transported me back to my teenage years.

Mom married my stepdad the same year as the recounted presidential election. We moved out of our apartment near the 24-hour carwash and into a house. From this deal, I got three stepsisters, an eventual younger brother, and a pool. My childhood "beach days" turned into self-conscious teenage "pool days."

On pool days, Mom divulged that, at my age, she had applied baby oil to tan. A baby-oil day in the sun for me would be like lying on the stove's burner. Mom looked like an Australian Gold spokesperson, and I looked like the son of Santa Claus. The cool kids in school were tan, so I ditched my SPF and started using bronzing lotion against the advice of the surgeon general. I soon pushed my luck and moved to tanning beds, which are coffins lined with ultraviolet lamps.

The idea of a tanning bed may sound over-the-top for someone with fair skin like me. But I was a teenager, and the future didn't exist. I bought a tanning bed membership, took off all my clothes to avoid tan lines, and closed the ultraviolet coffin's lid. I then refrained from moving for about seventeen to twenty minutes. One time I burnt my backside so crispy I couldn't sit properly for days. One might think a crispy backside would help me learn my lesson, but it didn't. I continued to (try) to tan until I moved to Orlando for college and started to spend all my tanning bed money on alcohol.

In college, I sometimes felt inclined to lie about my Florida-native status at parties. Remember, these parties took place in Florida, but two-thirds of the state's residents were born elsewhere. "Do you feel like people prejudge you because you're from Florida?" someone asked at one of these parties. I didn't have a chance to answer him. He launched into a therapy session about why he didn't like telling people he was from the Sunshine State. I understood his plight. I was a Floridian who couldn't tan. I could easily sell out my home state and pretend I'd grown up somewhere less weird, somewhere like the Midwest.

I graduated from college in 2010 and fulfilled my pasty, Midwest destiny. I relocated to Chicago, a city that called the shores of brutally cold Lake Michigan a beach. I loved it. Tan-ness wasn't a priority in a city covered by snow for nine months of the year. I made peace with my paleness. Unfortunately, I occasionally slipped up and told people I was from Florida. They met this admission with raised eyebrows and comments like, *Oh, the other day I saw the weirdest Florida Man story.* "Florida Man" had become the personification of weird Florida news stories, and the search term first spiked during the time I lived in Chicago. This correlation may or may not have been a coincidence. I'm going to leave Mr. Florida Man alone for now because he'll get his comeuppance from me later. I may have once hated the beach, but I hated Chicago winters even more. I eventually left the Windy City for graduate school somewhere warmer.

Things got complicated when I introduced myself to other graduate students enrolled in an MFA's Creative Nonfiction track. The group perked up when I admitted my Floridian roots because it's the land of mullet tossers and two bodies, one monkey. I had learned to keep my Florida childhood on the back burner, but as a nonfiction writer it's bad form to start off anything with a lie. I began a weird-stuff-happens spiel, but a smile stopped me. "I'm from Texas," said a big-haired blonde woman who looked like she was from Texas. "Crazy stuff happens in both our states. I'm used to it." Pride radiated from her whole body. The woman wore her state's stereotypes as a hard-fought badge of honor. I decided then and there to embrace Florida as I had my paleness years earlier.

I vowed to atone for my years spent in Florida denial.

Many people have denied things about Florida since it achieved statehood in 1845.

In 1878, the *Florida Agriculturist* ran the headline: "Where Do You Live and How Do You Live?" Transplants wanted to capitalize on agricultural promises like 300 bushels of sweet potatoes to the acre and $400 per acre for sugarcane. They were told they could stick an orange seed in the ground and wait for five years to have a grove worth $100 per tree. These sugarcane promises didn't all come true. Transplants spread "exaggerated stories to palm off some worthless tracts of land that were lakes in the rainy season and hot beds of malaria in the dry." The *Agriculturist* presented a call-to-action: "We request that those who have settled down here should give instructions [on how] people can live in Florida by their own labor, and the prospect for industrious people to prosper." The paper thought Floridians needed to tell their own stories to combat this negative reputation.

Today's Florida can be difficult to write about because there are many more Floridas now than there were in the 1800s. These Floridas exist throughout the long state. People call Miami "Little Cuba." There's the South in north Florida and Spanish influence in Tampa. More than 21 million people live in the state, and the Census report showed Florida's racial and ethnic makeup as 53.5 percent "white alone," 26.1 percent "Hispanic or Latino," and 16.9 percent "Black or African American alone." Florida's population makes it one of the country's most diverse states, but, as with anywhere in the United States, it has a history of racial issues.

In the late 1990s nearby St. Petersburg wanted to attract a Major League Baseball team. The City claimed eminent domain over black neighborhoods to build a stadium "without any real guarantee that baseball would come to the region at all." I was a kid then and excited to watch the Devil Rays, who have since dropped the Devil from their name. I didn't know their stadium continued a legacy of segregation. Decades earlier, the construction of an interstate served to divide the city by race. I didn't know that in 1914 there'd been a public lynching in the city, and a group of white men and women had "emptied their weapons for 10 minutes on the lifeless body."

A lot of the bad things people say about Florida are true. The state has a long history of racism, homophobia, drug/human/animal trafficking, wealth inequality, political scandals, notorious serial killers, and the list goes on (sometimes it's a wonder so many people still want to move here). There are real issues in the state that Floridians must continue to address. This book doesn't try to "defend" the state, but it does try to present a version of Florida other than the caricature so often seen in popular media. We've become so closely associated with outlandish stories that the real people who live here sometimes get overlooked. Residents are as complex as the state itself, and their stories are important for the future of both Florida and the United States. We're like the flamingo in the coal mine. As the Sunshine State goes, so goes the country.

I moved back home to write about some of Florida's polarizing people and its contradictions. I wanted to tell people that alligators are misunderstood. The reptiles are ferocious, but many animals rely on them to survive. In the dry season, they create mud burrows—gator holes—that fill with rainwater drunk by snakes, insects, turtles, and birds. I moonlight as a poet, remember, and this extended Florida-as-gator metaphor is to say: Floridians help us better understand the country's social, environmental, and political landscapes. This may be why certain people want to divorce Florida from the rest of the United States. They act like it's not a real place so they don't have to confront the state's realities.

Every Floridian has their own version of the state; this book is mine. It centers on the realities of Floridians I wanted to better understand. I'm most drawn to write about people I would meet in a halfway house, a drag queen's dressing room, or a gator pit. That must just be the Floridian in me because I spent time with all three while researching this book. Plus, I visited a rattlesnake room, a Confederate reenactment, and a clothing-optional campground. One thing I learned through my talks with Floridians—besides how to extract venom from a cobra—is that it's dangerous to meet our fears with fear. In this book, I've tried to face some of my fears—like the state's invasive species, environmental issues, hurricanes, and ghosts of the past.

I traveled around the state to meet an eclectic group of sometimes controversial Floridians. I chose these folks because I wanted to better understand them and how they shaped my version of Florida. In turn, they might help other Floridians understand their version of the state, too. I organized the book by perspectives on some of my Florida fears. To help tell these stories, I mixed interviews, archival research, and personal history. I talked to many more people than I could include in this book, and there are still so many Florida stories left to tell.

I have tried to escape Florida, but its land and people have always pulled me back home. I wrote this book for my fellow Floridians, those both proud and ashamed of our state. I also wrote it for the outsiders, the people who dream of a second chance and some sun. I wanted to show that even on its rough days—of which there are many—my home state's humanity transcends all those "because Florida" jokes.

ℱLORIDA MAN THEORY

I have a theory that any true Floridian is less than five degrees of separation from a Florida Man story, a headline like "Florida Man in Pirate Costume Arrested for Firing Black-Powder Guns." My theory rests on a Floridian knowing the neighbor's son, a "Florida Man Learns Hard Way That He Stole Laxatives, Not Opioids." Since Florida Man can also be Florida Woman, a Floridian might know a friend's cousin who went viral as "Florida Woman Charged with Stealing Rental Car Says 'Demons Took It.'" In my case, a family member called the cops when a drug deal went wrong. Her dealer tried to rob her, and she wanted him to get arrested. I found the pre-viral Florida Man story in one local newspaper. The story happened in the early 2000s, so it's all but buried on the internet.

In the mid-2000s, Fark.com—a website with the tagline "We Don't Make the News. We Mock It"—began to track weird Florida news and contributed to the genesis of Florida as an internet meme. A major increase in searches for the term "Florida Man" later occurred in June 2012, around the time of the viral Miami Cannibal story. A guy had reportedly smoked bath salts and chewed off the face of a homeless man who had passed out near a road. The Cannibal story was shocking, fear-inducing, twisted, and sad. The victim went through a slow and difficult recovery. The story was also morbidly intriguing to some, and it became a primer for Florida Man— who has been described as a "Yankee nightmare in human form" and "everything frightening about white trash life in one meme."

Florida Man entered the cultural zeitgeist soon after the cannibal story. An associate editor at *GQ* noticed the Florida attention and created the @_FloridaMan Twitter account to make his colleagues laugh. The account received nearly 64,000 followers its first month. The account used a mugshot of a man with black marker all over his face. This man was not an actual Florida Man, but a man arrested in Indiana for trying to "attack his roommate with a sword." The account's headlines contained an element of wildness, hopelessness, and physicality. Florida Man may have been out of control, but he had a certain ingenuity, often fueled by drugs and/or alcohol.

The internet loved these headlines and their accompanying mugshots. Florida Man may as well have been the mayor of Reddit with over a half million members in the subreddit dedicated to "news about the terrible superhero 'Florida Man' and his latest misadventures." He lodged himself into pop culture, depicted on the TV show *Atlanta*. He had his own beer, tour guide, and music festival once headlined by the indie rock band Weezer. He's apparently quite lucrative.

Journalist and author Craig Pittman interviewed me for a story he wrote about an attempt to trademark "Florida Man." I had written a book of Florida Man poems, and Craig wanted my thoughts on the guy who owned the aggregated site "floridaman.com." The site sold T-shirts and other merchandise. The owner had begun the process to trademark the term to thwart Oxygen TV. The network had announced a true crime show inspired by the meme. They described the show as when a crime is so outlandish that it "sounds like something from a Hollywood screenplay—there's a good chance it was actually committed by a 'Florida Man.'" The guy who owned the website "floridaman.com" wanted to trademark the term before the show aired. His attempt proved unsuccessful, but, hopefully, he won't try to sue me anyway.

Florida Man lived for about six years before his peak internet popularity. For the "Florida Man Challenge," sites like Twitter and Reddit encouraged people to Google their birthdates along with "Florida Man" to help people find their "inner Florida Man." The internet turned Florida Man into a Southern Gothic figure of indulgence, decadence, and bad decision making. That's a nice way of saying the meme allowed people to make fun of people who were often poor and dealing with addiction or mental health issues.

Floridians have never exactly maintained a pristine reputation. We've behaved badly since statehood. Historians called antebellum Florida a "rogue's paradise." Those Floridians liked to carry weapons, and "alcohol may have led to frontier violence." A penchant for alcohol and violence persisted and may have contributed to 1895's reported "Cutting Affray" when Chas stepped in front of Sam in line at the butcher shop. Sam's brother ran into the butcher shop to get a knife. He tried to stab Chas. The scrum lasted until "blood was seen" and the perpetrators fled to the woods to face later arrest.

I could almost understand fighting over a long wait for a good piece of meat, but I couldn't get down with a turn-of-the-century man who "Killed His Sweetheart." This story discussed a husband who asked his wife to "stroll by sunlight through the meadow and green pastures." On this stroll, the wife apparently told him she could no longer be with him "for all he is worth." Three shots were fired. The paper made it seem like the husband killed his wife, but the jury "held an inquest over the body," and "the verdict was that the shooting was accidental." They let him go.

Florida papers weren't always filled with such violence. There were sections for "fish news," poetry, potatoes, and the *Alachua Booster*'s "Edna May's recipe for being a successful wife to the ultra-rich." For those interested in bagging a sugar daddy, May's 1912 tips included spending time out in the country, focusing on vivacity, and living a simple life. I can't promise May's advice will translate to online dating success. During her time, Florida contained more alligators than people. Only about a half million folks lived in the state, a mostly untamed frontier. Businessmen and chamber of commerce members changed Florida's image. Developers dredged mangroves and salt marshes to make beaches. Trains brought people from up North. An 1896 advertisement for Tampa called the area a "health & pleasure seekers paradise," and a late-1800s article described its days as both invigorating and health restoring. The state marketed itself as a destination. The first sixty years of the twentieth century saw Florida's population balloon by more than 900 percent. Transplants brought with them their own ideas of paradise, and they had plenty of space to do generally weird things.

Generally weird Florida emerged as a news subgenre, in part, because beach bum life coexisted alongside diverse flora and profitable fauna like the reported "Wave of Palm Tree Thefts" in the mid-1990s. Former *Tampa Bay Times* editor Janet Keeler told me that generally weird headlines evolved into "Florida Man" because of journalism basics. The inverted pyramid put the most important information at the beginning of a news story, and, for decades, journalists refrained from using everyday people's names in leads, the first sentence or two of stories. This meant stories often started with "Florida man arrested for" or "Florida woman arrested for," and, Keeler said, "without this construction social media wouldn't have such a tidy way to collect the stories." These news headlines helped Florida man become Florida Man, but the state's bad behavior may have stayed regionally confined, like, say, Idaho's or Nebraska's news, if not for our public record laws.

Craig Pittman mentioned these laws during a "Who Is 'Florida Man'" segment on *The Daily Show with Trevor Noah*. "Florida was the first state in the nation to pass this landmark law called the Sunshine Act," he said. "Basically, any government document is available for reporters to go in and see." Florida Man may live on the internet, but his crimes occurred in real life. I had wanted to understand these sunshine laws better, so I emailed Professor Catherine Cameron at the Stetson University College of Law. "That Florida Man," she responded, "certainly does get himself into a lot of trouble!"

On the day of our interview, I kept my engine running in the parking lot of Florida's oldest law school. I listened to a DJ break down the day's news. A Florida man had been arrested for allegedly carrying a Molotov cocktail for his own protection. "Of course, that story happened in Florida," the DJ said. "We do the news best down here." He laughed. Thunder rumbled. Storms had raged so badly the previous day that administrators threatened to cancel classes. As quickly as the Florida rain came, so it went. I didn't need an umbrella as I walked to Professor Cameron's office.

We had both spent our formative years in Pinellas County. The area inspired 2012's *Spring Breakers*, and scenes were filmed in the same city as Stetson Law. In the sex-and-drug-fueled film, James

Franco sported iconic Florida tattoos such as a gun, the state's outline, and my hometown's 727 area code. He embodied everything I once considered cool, and if I could've gotten similar tattoos as a young teen, I probably would have. Professor Cameron looked less like the tatted Franco and more like the clean-cut Blossom, a friendly TV character from the nineties who grew up to be Dr. Amy Farrah Fowler on *The Big Bang Theory*.

Lawyers make certain Floridians uncomfortable, but our shared Florida-ness and her relaxed demeanor put me at ease. She had studied journalism, communication, and law at the University of Florida, then fled to the North to work at the Reporters Committee for Freedom of the Press in Washington, D.C. "It is quite the stigma when you live elsewhere that you're from Florida," she said. "They think everyone down here is crazy." Professor Cameron eventually moved back to the Sunshine State for a job and to live closer to family.

She told me internet writers took to our WTF(lorida) moments because of our reputation, and because our laws made it easy to access reports. A push for public record law reform came after the Watergate scandal in the 1970s, when President Richard Nixon got caught in a string ball of lies journalists helped unravel. People wanted more public accountability. Citizens funded the government and wanted access to governmental actions and information. We should know everything from our leaders' on-the-record discussions of reality TV to their plans for using taxpayer funds. Most states opened the records but balanced them against privacy rights. Florida basically said, *it's whatever*. Anything's fair game.

Florida passed laws nicknamed sunshine because, as anyone raised in the church like me knew, what was done in the dark eventually came to the light. The nickname also led to questionable legal writing puns like the laws "can cause sunburn." Puns aside, these laws helped Florida become the state to which many other states looked for their own open government statutes. Florida developed a broad presumption of openness in public record laws. Journalists and bloggers and anyone else could access public documents. These documents included police reports that could be turned into clickbait headlines.

The full Florida Man story may go untold because of the fast-paced news cycle paired with specific exemptions. These public records exemptions created a lag between the initial information available and the facts needed to tell a full story. One of these exemptions allowed records to be sealed for active, ongoing investigations. This allowed officers to do their jobs. It also meant journalists got blurbs from police blotters without getting much else. "If you could wait until after the investigation," said Professor Cameron, "then you'd have the complete story, and I wonder if that's the discrepancy between what ends up in the headline and what really happened to these folks." Writers couldn't get immediate access to the full information, but they could get a headline and a mugshot.

These mugshots weren't only used by journalists. Websites began to publish booking photos and charged a fee for people who wanted them removed. One of these sites allegedly took more than $2.4 million in fees from nearly six thousand people nationwide. A group filed a class-action lawsuit against such sites because of their exploitation. Journalists might not use these photos for the same kind of exploitation, but a story's mugshot identifies a person as no good. The person's guilt didn't necessarily matter. Those who survived high school can attest: the truth doesn't always save a tarnished reputation.

It may seem like I'm against such laws, but Florida's public records are a source of state pride. We should be able to keep tabs on public officials. We should also be able to access these records to screen our first dates. These laws are good things, but they are also a reason why Florida Man became an easy joke.

The records in states like California and Arizona are nearly as open as Florida's own. And I'm calling it now. Arizona will be the next Florida. People move there for retirement, odd desert reptiles abound, and they keep their public records open. Arizona Man may one day reign as king over the weird news game, but, for now, it's still Florida Man. He's the usual and easiest suspect.

Before I left Professor Cameron's office, she mentioned a cultural shift. She believed we've been allowed to distance ourselves from people in headlines who sometimes got fired for their public mugshots. Some reportedly killed themselves after struggling with the infamy. "It's a cultural phenomenon that we don't recognize that these are real people," she said. "The infotainment part of journalism made us all forget that this is not an actor on TV. This is an actual human being and a life."

I talked to my best friend from high school, Jessica, about my Florida Man Theory. We met in sophomore year at a Southern Baptist high school. She told me after graduation she thought we'd cliqued up because she was one of the school's only students of color, and I was one of its only closeted gay ones. We have remained close as adults. I figured between the two of us we could come up with a Florida Man for me to interview. I wanted to write about the Florida Man phenomenon from an insider's point of view. Most stories wrote about Florida Man in the abstract, but few, if any at that point, had talked to an actual person from the headline. I wanted to hear from someone whose arrest headline had gone viral and spread across the internet like hot gossip. I wanted to hear the what-happened-next.

"Oh," Jessica said, "I have two people who'd be perfect."

One of these two had moved to somewhere normal like Connecticut, but the other, Rachel Hayes, lived a few hours south of us in Fort Lauderdale. I had never met Rachel, but we both, like Professor Cameron, had grown up in Pinellas County. Rachel made headlines in 2014 as "Florida Woman Repeatedly Slapped Her Grandmother for Rejecting Her Friend Request on Facebook." On one of these articles, a commenter wrote, "You could have left out any references to Pinellas County and people would still know this happened in Pinellas County." The article's author responded, "True; Pinellas County is the Florida of Florida."

"I don't know if Rachel will be open to talking about it," Jessica said. "It was pretty messy, but I'll send her a message on Facebook."

Rachel initially expressed some hesitation. I was the first media person to reach out to her, and I learned early on journalists must get used to people not liking them. Those in the field need to be persistent, or sometimes to badger, to the point of annoyance. A journalism professor once told me if I wanted to be popular then I needed to find another job. "Journalists," he said, "drink blood and eat nails for breakfast." I never acquired the taste for blood or nails, but I knew skin in the game could help.

I told Rachel that at eighteen, I had driven home wasted from a gay nightclub in Tampa. I partied in the city because it stood far enough away from home to hide me from my parents and God. The night of my arrest, I noticed police lights behind me somewhere on a Tampa interstate. I pulled off the road and into a mall parking lot. My breathalyzer test showed a blood alcohol content nearly three times the legal limit for drivers twenty-one and over. I spent the night in jail and passed out in the drunk tank. I later received a sentence of fines, probation, and alcohol treatment.

I used to tell that story and say I drank so much because I was struggling with my sexuality and eternal damnation. I was struggling, but I can now say I am also a textbook alcoholic who hails from a long line of addicts. I quit drinking-and-driving after my arrest, but I didn't quit drinking, not even during my court-mandated outpatient rehab. I didn't think teenagers could be alcoholics. I thought that was for people in, like, their forties. I couldn't imagine life without booze—my closest friend and giver of personality. I finally stopped drinking about five years after my arrest. I still thought I was too young to be an alcoholic, but my options were to either give up drinking or stay trying to piece together blackout nights. I have years of recovery now, and I'd like to think my personality—and decision-making skills—have only gotten better.

My arrest didn't get blasted all over the news and social media like Rachel's had. Her mugshot received BBC levels of attention. The alleged WWE Grandma Smackdown even made its way to Nancy Grace, the TV commentator who had once obsessed over Florida's Casey Anthony. Nancy called Rachel an unfit mother. "It bothered me that Nancy Grace could be so negative and nasty about me," Rachel said. "I knew that if this was her opinion, she'd sway a lot of other people's opinion about me." The whole world seemed to make fun of her for clicks.

People ridiculed in the media don't always want to chat with reporters like me who drink blood. But after I told Rachel my story, my skin in the game, she extended an invitation to visit her in Fort Lauderdale, where she lived in a halfway house for women.

Rachel looked much healthier in 2015 than she did in her viral mugshot from the previous year. That photo showed her with stringy brown hair, and I was surprised to see a blonde with pink and teal streaks. I met the twenty-seven-year-old during her shift at a Primanti Bros. sandwich shop across from Fort Lauderdale Beach.

Primanti Bros. occupied a prime spot on A1A, a state road that hugged the Atlantic Ocean. I had never heard of the 24-hour chain, but it started in Pittsburgh and migrated south like many northerners. The restaurant stood near several gift shops that sold a mix of neon tank tops and T-shirts with bad puns like "FBI: Female Body Inspector." People found their way to Primanti Bros. after a night of drinking. Rachel took their orders, filled glasses of soda, and helped an arguing couple with their A1A directions issues.

Rachel worked fifty hours over the week with shifts from midnight to 6:00 a.m. or 8:00 p.m. to 6:00 a.m. She described the job as humbling. She had made about fifty thousand dollars a year as a server on Clearwater Beach. She had spent most of her off-time with her boyfriend; they rode around on a motorcycle and drank on the famous beach. At the sandwich shop, she found a sort of roughneck camaraderie with her coworkers. The guys watched out for her, unlike at her first job in the city at a telemarketing place. A former coworker Googled her name and found her mugshot. She had moved to Fort Lauderdale for a fresh start, but her coworker called her a Facebook grandma beater in front of other employees. She quit. "The whole thing was humiliating, and I didn't want to show my face anywhere," said Rachel. "It didn't even happen because of Facebook."

In 2014, Rachel's mom had driven her to dinner at Grandma's place on the fateful night of her viral arrest. Rachel couldn't drive that night because she'd previously been arrested for DUI and public urination. Such charges, unfortunately, are not so uncommon for those in the throes of addiction. Because of these charges, she sold her car and began to ride a bicycle around town until she got hit by a car. This accident left Rachel in a wheelchair for a while. Her drinking got worse. She arranged for her five-year-old son to spend Christmas with family. She didn't want him to see her drunk during the holidays. They planned a final meal at Grandma's.

Rachel's mom, Rebecca, told me dinner was going fine until the night took a dramatic turn. Rachel had snapped a group photo and went to post it to Facebook. She tried to tag her grandmother in the post, but she couldn't. Her grandmother informed Rachel she'd unfriended her on the social media platform. Rachel had changed her name on Facebook to include the word "Freakin" as a joke. But her grandmother didn't find it funny. The two didn't have the best relationship for a while. They didn't see eye-to-eye on some of Rachel's life choices, mainly money issues and the type of guys she dated.

Rachel's grandmother didn't want her doctor and lawyer friends to see Rachel's Freakin name. It embarrassed her.

The "you're embarrassing" part of the statement escalated this argument to Florida Man proportions. "My mother pushed Rachel," said Rebecca. "It was so confusing and happening so fast. It turned into a big nightmare." As many do in times of crisis, Rachel went outside to smoke a cigarette. She decided to go home.

After her cigarette, she went back inside her grandmother's house to get her son. Rachel had been drinking, and her family didn't want her son going anywhere. I've never physically fought with family members, but I know the feeling of being you-can't-tell-me-anything drunk. Rachel was angry and pushed her grandmother, who, Rachel said, went on the offensive. Her grandmother, "about six foot, one inch and very German," allegedly pushed the five-foot, two-inch Rachel. She got Rachel out of the front door and locked it.

Rachel went to the next logical location: a bar.

She eventually found her way home. In the wee hours of the morning, police officers knocked on her apartment door. They told Rachel her grandmother had reported the confrontation. They arrested her. She spent a night in jail for violent offenders. "I was so scared," she said. "I felt like I didn't belong there." The next day, text messages flooded her phone.

What happened?

Is this real?

Are you OK?

At first, she didn't understand these messages, but she logged onto Facebook and saw the posts. She'd made international headlines as a grandma beater. "I never, ever thought anything like that would happen to me," she said. "It all started from whatever this officer put in a police report."

Rachel had never seen the arrest affidavit cited by media outlets. I wanted to read the exact wording that led to the viral "Granny Beater" headlines, so I went to get a copy. Florida made it easy to do this. I logged onto the county clerk's website, typed in a name, and, voila, an icon popped up: Order Documents! Click Here! Request Now! Including Certified! I didn't even need to put on clothes to get Rachel's arrest documents, but I wanted to go old school. I trekked down to the Pinellas County courthouse, Florida Man's mothership. I hadn't visited this courthouse much in the nearly ten years since my own arrest. The place made me nervous, but I bolted into its air-conditioning and took my place in line for the metal detector.

The courthouse divided the records into a station for misdemeanors and another for felonies. I stopped at the misdemeanor counter to get my own affidavit. The clerk joked about the weekend and smiled throughout the process. I saw my file and immediately blurted, "So much has changed since then." I wanted to give this clerk the lengthy backstory I had recited many times. I stopped myself. I figured she didn't need to hear another movie of the week about a Florida teen in a dark place who drank too much and got arrested in a mall parking lot. In that moment, my mind went to Rachel. She didn't always have the option of keeping the past to herself.

I moved on to the felony counter and gave the less-friendly felony clerk Rachel's case number. I paid three dollars to get the documents, and I held the typed-out statement:

> This evening def was at vic's residence when they got into an argument because the vic would not accept the def's Facebook request. In the midst of the argument the def slapped the victim multiple times on the side of her face without the victim's permission. The victim is 72 years old.

This statement led to a slew of page views, but there's no telling how many journalists or bloggers referenced it for their stories. The digital media landscape made it acceptable to quote another media outlet without looking at the original source. This made stories sound like a game of telephone. Information got distorted or dropped altogether. He heard it from her, who heard it from him, who can't remember where he heard it. Some stories had made it sound like Rachel jumped her grandmother in a Facebook Territory War. They described her as a *Mortal Kombat* character whose Fatality move came as a flurry of slaps. But that's not exactly how things went down.

Rachel's mom told me the argument was a family dispute that had been boiling for a while and one that should have never made the news. She wished they had been able to keep their family disagreements quiet.

☀

A few days after her story went viral, Rachel boarded a Greyhound bus. It was New Year's Eve, and people around her toasted the good life as she headed to rehab. Everyone but her seemed filled with hope. Rachel wanted to disappear. Few people want to go to rehab, even one located near a famous beach.

I met Rachel nearly a full year after she arrived in Fort Lauderdale. The felony charge of "elder abuse" from the family dinner had long been dropped. A judge never saw the case. "It's not like I hit or punched my grandmother," she said. We sat in her screened-in porch at an all-women sober house. The residents had to abide by rules and a curfew; they paid rent, completed chores, attended meetings, submitted to drug tests, and maintained a job. Most residents shared a room. It was like dorm life except without blacked-out nights full of tears (at least that was my college experience).

The porch's air-conditioning unit hummed. Sun shone through the screen. A pot of Venus flytraps, carnivorous plants, stood on a windowsill. Rachel lit a cigarette. "I had a fall from grace," she said. "My boyfriend was cute, and we were drinking on the beach." She got caught up in the Florida vacation lifestyle, full of rum runners and piña coladas. I could relate to the vacation life she referred to, but she put Floridian life in terms I had never considered. "Think about it," she said. "Say you live in Alabama, and you work all year just to have one week in Florida. There's drinking. There's partying. We don't ever have to do that. We don't ever have to work the whole year to get this Florida life." Rachel didn't blame Florida for her alcoholism, but the year-round spring break atmosphere warped her sense of reality. "I think being born in Florida is almost like being born into a royal family," she said. "You may take it for granted and can be real fucked up because of it."

I had been sober for nearly four and a half years when I talked to Rachel, and our conversation turned to the steps of her recovery. AA is anonymous, but she made it clear she wanted me to let people know she was in it because the program helped save her life. Rachel described her initial weeks of treatment as hell. She was a mess and had problems with authority. One of the longtime residents told me Rachel talked "5,000 miles a minute" when she first arrived at the halfway house and was full of anxiety. Another resident described

Rachel's progress as impressive and called her "an inspiration to us all."

Rachel's roommate opened the screen door to hand her a piece of mail. Her roommate, blonde and softball player–esque, recently moved to Florida from North Carolina. The two had become close friends. They stocked up on junk food and watched scary movies every Thursday night.

"Yes!" Rachel said after she opened the mail. "I can finally have a normal bank account." A Florida Man lifestyle can mess up your record and also your credit. The bank put Rachel on a year of probation, and she couldn't do much with her finances. The letter confirmed a positive evaluation and meant she could open a normal bank account.

The two of us left the screened-in porch for a tour of the grounds. Rachel completed community service for her DUI, in part, through maintenance around this halfway house. "I planted all these," she said and pointed to small bushes. "I tried to water this whole side. I wanted it to look nice." We walked through the courtyard, and a cat named Sylvester scurried by us. Rachel had settled into a quiet life, but her Florida Woman headline would most likely never get scrubbed. The internet won't let anyone forget anything. Ever. "There's still a big battle in my head," she said. "What if I meet someone? Do I tell them upfront? Everybody's first instinct is to look it up."

Rachel never deleted her Facebook account, but she did remove the "Freakin" from her name. She used the social network that almost ruined her life to tell her story. Her status updates often involved recovery messages. Instead of posts tagged with her mugshot, she received messages from people who wanted help getting sober. In a recent Facebook post she wrote, "If you would have told me a year and a half ago that this would be my life, I dunno lol I would have probably tried to fight you. [But now,] I'm able to share my story with the world without embarrassment." Her grandmother, who later accepted her friend request, can see all these posts. The two have since mended fences. They tag each other in photos, all clear eyes and smiles.

*O*F THE STORM

The oldest oak tree in my grandmother's front yard dropped a heavy branch on her house as 2017's Category 5 Hurricane Irma approached Florida. I had finished graduate school and moved back in with my grandmother, who I call Gramel ("gra" plus her initials MEL). I heard the thunder-loud crack of the tree from my childhood bedroom. I rushed out to the yard. The branch hadn't completely split from the tree; it balanced on the roof's lip. As a journalist, I knew I needed to take immediate action, but I'm also a poet who didn't own a full set of tools. My stepdad brought over his toolbox, and I put on gloves and goggles. I looked the part as we tried to *Texas Chainsaw Massacre* the branch. This task proved too dangerous for us, so I Googled tree services and found a phone number for a tree man, who showed up a few hours later. He pronounced the tree diseased. The oak had rotted from the inside. He said it should've been cut down years earlier.

I had grown up a tree-climber, and this oak was my favorite. As a child, I maneuvered my body up its branches. I stretched my arms to find footholds. I could climb this oak higher than anyone I knew, higher than the boy from church I climbed trees with until he said I sounded gay. I had pressed my hands to branches to feel strong, and I climbed as high and as often as I could. Air felt cooler up in the leaves than on the frying-pan ground. I wanted to see everything the tree saw. Tippy-top branches, slimmer than the lower ones, couldn't hold me up. On brave days, I tried my luck to look past our neighborhood with its paved roads and houses. This landscape looked different from what Mom would have seen when she climbed this tree.

I pictured dirt mounds and the nearby lake where she and my uncle caught tadpoles and "fungus de-munges."

I couldn't help but see Gramel's diseased tree as a metaphor for my own mortality. But it was most certainly not a metaphor. It was, as Gramel described it, a "big freakin" dead tree. I needed to get it cut down. To do this properly, homeowners in my city had to first fill out an application found online. They needed to include a drawing of where the tree stood on the property. A hand-drawn diagram would work, but the submitter had to include the tree type proposed for removal. Certain types of trees such as pecan, slash pine, live oak, and bald cypress required replacement after removal. Mangroves were not supposed to be uprooted for any reason. The City could also send out workers to create a plan for the tree's removal. This process could take weeks or months and sometimes thousands of dollars. Failure to follow protocol—or at least getting caught not following protocol—could result in fines.

I had tried to become a rule follower as an adult, and I also worked part time for the City in its Department of Recreation, Parks and Arts. I knew to follow protocol, but Hurricane Irma was making a beeline for Gramel's house. And we had a big freakin' tree branch problem. I skipped protocol. The first tree man told us the thick oak would either fall directly on the house or into the street if Irma's projected 170-mile-per-hour winds blew through our neighborhood. He said even if a hurricane didn't hit the tree, it would eventually fall. He offered to bring a big truck with an elevating bucket to solve our problem for $1,500, which, upon later research, seems fair. Probably even cheap. Gramel lived on a fixed income, and I worked three part-time jobs at the time, so we weren't swimming in money. Irma circled out in the ocean about a week away, and I figured the hurricane's distance allowed us enough time to bargain-shop. I've often been called frugal, even cheap.

I had grown up with hurricanes and was used to them. Their names sounded like my fellow church boys: Matthew, Andrew, and Charley. We'd gone days without power for those storms. I had stepped over fallen power lines as I walked down our street. In college, hurricanes presented an opportunity to get day drunk during canceled classes, or, as we called them, Florida snow days.

My hometown area hadn't experienced a direct hit since 1921, but the weatherman told us Irma could change our luck. The history of recorded hurricanes dates to Christopher Columbus. The explorer weathered "a vicious storm that looks to have been a hurricane" not too far from modern-day Florida. Some hurricanes started as easterly waves off the coast of Africa, and others began in the Caribbean or Gulf. Florida was often in their path, and the warm water of the Gulf Stream allowed hurricanes to intensify near the state. These mad, furious winds had hit Florida more than any other state, nearly five hundred times since 1851. One of the state's deadliest storms occurred in 1928. The storm battered Palm Beach with strong winds as it made its way toward central Florida's Lake Okeechobee. Back then, people didn't have spaghetti models with their squiggly neon lines to track the storm's potential paths. The storm's initial reports seemed heartening for Floridians until the communication was restored and "long lists of dead and injured began trickling through." This storm later became known as "The Great Hurricane of 1928," and Zora Neale Hurston wrote about it in *Their Eyes Were Watching God*. Agencies estimated around 2,500 Floridians died during this hurricane, but modern historians believe the death toll to be higher.

Reports on Irma predicted the storm could be larger than the Great Hurricane. Floridians all over the state began to prepare for the worst. I worked as an adjunct writing teacher at a local college, and one of my students told me she went to Walmart to find bottled water for her newborn. The store ran dry, and she started to cry in an aisle. A woman walked up to her and handed my student a case from her own cart. "I felt so relieved," my student said. This student then asked me for suggestions on her rough draft because she planned to work on it if she didn't lose power. Her resiliency amazed me.

At another one of my jobs, for the City, I was told I'd be listed as a second responder. The first responders were full-time employees, and they were to be stationed at one of the City's shelters during the storm. They would work in eight-hour shifts and take naps in back areas. As a second responder, I needed to show up early in the morning after the storm passed to help with the damage.

In the meantime, I tried to get Gramel's house hurricane ready. My best friend from high school, Jessica, and her two kids lived about five minutes from Gramel's house. Jessica had always been a DIY kind of person, which benefited me. She put together furniture I bought online, owned a drill set, and once tried to install her own drywall. As the storm barreled our way, she helped me board up Gramel's windows with rippled waves of metal sheets. We didn't talk much as we worked. We both felt more anxiety about this storm than any before it. Jessica finished the work and left to search for a generator in another county as all those in ours had reportedly been sold.

The metal sheets turned Gramel's house into a cave, and they turned us into bats. We knew what happened outside those windows by sound. I didn't want to venture outside our hiding place.

Some Floridians like me hid from hurricanes, but others like Morgan Guigon ran to them. As a child, Morgan acted like a weather reporter. While I spent my childhood climbing trees, he spent his shooting home videos of brewing tropical storms. He watched Helen Hunt and Bill Paxton chase storms in *Twister*, and he wanted to turn his childhood passion into a career. He began to study meteorology in college and chased random pop-up thunderstorms. After two years in college, he switched his major to business because he "got a lot more business than meteorology." He chased his first hurricane in 2005 when Hurricane Wilma made landfall on Florida's west coast.

In 2013, he and a friend founded the South Florida Storm Chasers. The group grew to about thirty-five storm chasers with backgrounds that ranged from college students to retired TV meteorologists. During this time, storm chasers could make good money from their videos. They could shop them around to channels who wanted exclusive rights. Cell-phone cameras changed the game. "Now, any storm or tornado gets shot by ten different people," said Morgan. Outlets wanted to contract chasers.

Morgan still chased, even with diminishing monetary returns. He tracked storms through the website Tropical Tidbits. His go-kit consisted of a three-day supply of waterproof clothes plus a full medical kit. He chased in a 2012 Chevrolet Suburban equipped with hurricane-resistant glass windows and reinforced door handles. He also packed ropes and chains so he could "get out of sticky situations." He told me he didn't worry about outside forces in his vehicle. I took his word for it because I'd never be the one to run toward a storm. I didn't have the legs for it. Storm chasing hadn't stopped exhilarating him, but the damage he saw had affected him. Storm chasers experienced a hurricane's carnage firsthand, and sometimes they felt powerless to help. Three famous storm chasers died in the field chasing a tornado Morgan had chased, too. He began to see his role as more of a first responder and educator.

He had chased many storms before Irma, but Morgan decided to sit out the Category 5 hurricane. The storm threatened to make landfall near his home in south Florida, and it looked like a worst-case scenario situation. "I could have either spent my time forecasting or preparing my home," he said. "I decided to make sure my home and family were safe."

To make sure my family was safe, I needed to get Gramel's dead oak tree cut down. We found a phone number in the local paper for a new tree guy. I looked him up online, and he seemed legit. Almost. I'll leave out certain parts of this story because they're most likely illegal. Not go-to-prison illegal. More like pay-fines illegal. But still.

The new tree guy arrived around nightfall. He looked like so many men I'd grown up around, like a white guy from a rap video. He was lean, covered in tattoos and cigarette stains. In a past life, I might have been attracted to him. He examined the oak and said he could get the job done the next morning. He'd do it for six hundred dollars. Only accepted cash. The tree guy looked rough, but he seemed respectful enough. He addressed Gramel as ma'am. She and I speculated he might need cash for drugs. We decided it was none of our business how he spent his money.

Plus, we couldn't find anyone to do the job for cheaper. It seemed like everyone needed a tree man as the storm loomed only a few days away. The news told of price gouging and warned of scammers like unlicensed contractors who'd done work on roofs, driveways, and, yes, trees. People panicked. Facebook friends updated each other on gas stations sold out of gas. No one knew for sure where the storm would land. We just knew it would.

Gramel and I should have probably evacuated or gone to a shelter, but both of us wanted to stay put. Gramel felt bad about leaving the oak unattended. She said she could deal with the tree falling on her house, but what if it fell onto somebody else's? How could she live with that? The weatherman said this was our big storm, and as it got closer, I believed him. I began to take pictures of the rooms in

Gramel's house so we could show these pictures to insurance agents if we lost everything.

The next morning the tattooed tree guy came on-time-ish with a partner. He wrapped ropes around his skinny torso and scaled the oak I'd so often climbed as a kid. He wore a leather tool belt with a chainsaw hooked by a carabiner. I watched as he used a series of ropes to shimmy into the sky. He cranked the chainsaw to cut off branches, then lowered these branches down to his partner. The tree guy worked methodically. Gracefully. Still, I almost had like sixteen heart attacks throughout this process. I swore he would drop one of those heavy limbs on the house, and it would go right through the roof. The tree guy said his safety was on the line, too. He told me he'd go down with a dropped tree branch, and that it was all about geometry. But I've never been the best at math. His calculations were our only hope.

About midday, he and his partner took a break. They smoked cigarettes inside his truck with the air-conditioning on. Gramel offered them "cool drinks" as she does to anyone who visited her house. They declined. They had brought their own. The men finished their drinks and cigarettes and focused on the tree. Its branches were scattered like toothpicks. A few hours later they finished, and the tree guy pulled Gramel's mailbox out of the ground to put the cut branches near the road. I paid him, and he left.

The debris created a wall. Our across-the-street neighbor confronted us about it. She told me it could be dangerous for her family and that we shouldn't have cut down the tree. I understood her concerns. Palpable anxiety spread over the state. Gramel and I talked over whether we'd done the right thing. "I would feel awful if anything happens to them because of me," she said. The neighbor's husband called us later that night. He demanded Gramel give him the phone number for the tree guy. He'd seen more news stories of tree men who had taken advantage of people. Gramel didn't want to give him the number because the tree guy had helped us out. She also felt a bit salty that our neighbor thought she was "just some little old lady" who'd let someone take advantage of her. She gave him the number anyway.

Before the storm hit, the City came by our house with one of those street-long garbage trucks. It took them two full trips to finish collecting the debris, and the guy in charge wasn't too happy with us. I felt bad to use their resources when so many other people needed their help, but I was relieved they took our debris before the hurricane. A little while later, our house phone rang. It wasn't my neighbor's husband like I expected. It was the tree guy. He was angry and told me the husband had threatened to call the news to get his business shut down and have him arrested. "I did you all a favor," the tree guy said. "Now, I might lose everything because of it." I apologized and thanked him for his help. I felt he might have saved our house and Gramel's life. I wanted him to know I appreciated his work. "I wish I wouldn't have done it," he said. The tree guy had been so nice, but I understood. I also understood he knew where we lived and that he could roll up on the house with his tattoos and partner whenever he wanted. I apologized again, and he hung up.

That night, the metal shutters Jessica helped me put up banged against the windows as Irma raged. I thought the roof would fly off at any minute. Gramel and I lit candles. We prayed. The power went out across the city. I'd never felt more connected to Floridians across the state than during the storm. I imagined they, like me, were thinking about if they had it in them to rebuild everything.

After the storm, the old oak became a large stump on which Gramel placed holiday decorations: green on St. Patrick's Day, a fake jack-o-lantern for Halloween. The man who cut down the tree never called us again. Neither did our neighbors. Gramel had known them for decades, but they never talked to us again after Irma. Eventually, a younger couple moved into the house. Gramel said she'll never ride out another big hurricane. She hated even the mention of storms.

My younger brother John held a different stance. He has always followed the weather. He used to tell me the day's high and let me know when it was going to rain. He marked hurricane season on his calendar and watched videos of storm chasers on YouTube.

Two hurricane seasons after Irma, John showed me a YouTube video titled *Hurricane Irma—the Damage*. The YouTubers discussed their storm preparations and their lives in the aftermath. The monstrous Irma brought comparatively little damage to our area, but severely hit other parts of Florida. The recovery proved slow and ongoing. Irma destroyed an estimated 25 percent of the buildings in the Keys. About one thousand homes sustained major damage in Miami-Dade County. The agricultural industry reported a loss of nearly $245 million.

Most of the storm's direct deaths occurred in the Caribbean; people drowned or were struck by lightning. Seventy-seven Floridians died "indirectly" due to falls, accidents, carbon monoxide poisoning, and electrocutions. An eighty-nine-year-old man drowned in a canal. Twelve people died in a nursing home when the building lost power, and it became sweltering. Wind knocked over an eighty-six-year-old man who fatally hit his head.

Nearly 6.8 million Floridians left their homes for Irma in the largest mass exodus in U.S. history. Then governor Rick Scott had declared a state of emergency. He ordered people in fifty-four of Florida's sixty-seven counties to evacuate. Dr. Jennifer Collins had written articles and books on the state's weather, and she wanted to figure out why certain Floridians stayed put for the storm.

Dr. Collins surveyed evacuees from Hurricane Matthew, another Category 5 hurricane that affected Florida. People who stayed for Matthew had a good local support network of neighbors and friends. Irma produced different results. Those evacuees tried to get completely out of the state, not just to a different part of it. They met standstill traffic on the interstate and already booked hotels in neighboring states. Dr. Collins said some of this panic could have been avoided with a hurricane plan. Many people didn't have one. They'd either recently moved to the state or had lived in Florida their whole lives without being severely affected by a hurricane. Florida's location lent it to being hit by a hurricane. Climate change had caused sea levels to rise, and storm surge now pushes more water onto land. "We just need that one, and you're done," said Collins. "It will hit Tampa. It's a matter of time. It's not if, it's when." The state's coast is vulnerable along with its large population of elderly folks. "It's about thinking about your network and not being afraid to ask for help," she said. "People want to help out in times of crisis, and it's really important to have those networks."

I'd once talked about hurricanes as if they were nothing more than casual rainstorms. Like we could ever be more powerful than them. Like they didn't wipe out everything people had work their whole lives to get. The meaning of hurricanes can be people trapped in attics as the water rushed toward them. There were people who stayed for the storm because they had nowhere else to go. Networks can be difficult to form as most people who live in Florida weren't born here. They haven't had as much time to build up their community.

Still, Floridians who lived through Irma and hurricanes before it hadn't been alone. We heard those storms together. We heard them and told ourselves we would help each other in the aftermath. We told ourselves the next hurricane wouldn't destroy us, and neither would the next storm or the one after that.

A CONFEDERACY
OF REENACTORS

People have told me Florida is just Disney World or beaches or old people. They usually don't associate the state with the South like they do Georgia or Mississippi. Those states couldn't shake the South; it was heard in *bless your heart* voices. Florida's current place in the American consciousness may not include the South, but its past does.

A Florida convention voted 62 yeas and 7 nays to secede after the presidential election of Abraham Lincoln in 1860 and became the third state to join the Confederacy. Florida's population totaled around 140,000 people. About half of its citizens were enslaved black people. Most of those enslaved people worked on plantations in the northern part of Florida, where they tilled cotton, tobacco, and corn as well as vegetables like squash. The convention said a push for secession centered on the "rapid spread of Northern fanaticism" and its encroachment on the state's "liberties and institutions." The convention's white, land-owning male voters decided these liberties included their ability to enslave people. Florida has been called the "forgotten state of the Civil War." I never learned much in school about the state's role in a war that saw upward of 850,000 deaths. The Florida history I learned was the disputed legend of Ponce de León's search for the Fountain of Youth, which my grandparents took me to visit in St. Augustine when I was a kid. Still, I found a baby bib with my name stitched below a Confederate flag in one of my keepsake boxes.

I didn't think much about what it meant to be a southerner until the Confederate flag baby bib. My Florida-born Granny Lula called us southern, and that was good enough for me. She told me stories of her brother sticking a pitchfork through the outhouse seat when she was trying to use it. She had cut heads off chickens before she cooked them. Granny fixed us collard greens and cornbread. We drank sweet tea with no lemon. I didn't need any other proof of our southern-ness.

I'm a fifth-generation Floridian, and I realize there's a difference between a "Floridian" who wears flip-flops all year, shops at the grocery chain Publix, and thinks 70 degrees is cold and a "southerner." But the two identities can cross. The Florida-southerner can be most often found in north Florida. People describe the Panhandle as south Alabama. I've also seen Confederate flag beach towels sold in Fort Lauderdale gift shops. I connected to the South through my family food and their stories. I expanded my southern pursuit in college. I read southern literature, studied history, and bought cowboy boots. On a first date, a guy who grew up in Tallahassee told me none of my efforts made me any more southern. "If you didn't eat squirrel as a kid," he said, "then you're not a southerner." People like this first-date guy got serious about who could and couldn't identify as a southerner. I'd never eaten squirrel or completed other arbitrary markers, so I often didn't make the cut. (For the record, I most definitely did not go on a second date with the squirrel-eater. Not because he ate squirrels, but because he was rude.)

I began to question why I even cared about identifying as a southerner. I stopped seeing the point of aligning myself with a history synonymous, for some, with racism, homophobia, and oppression. Floridians didn't have to identify as southern. People can't—bless their hearts—hear it in most of our voices. I could deny these southern roots like I once had with Florida. It can be beneficial to deny the South, but some Floridians choose a different approach.

On a Saturday morning in 2019, twelve Civil War reenactors stood shoulder-to-shoulder in the Brooksville woods, about an hour from Tampa. The first rays of sunlight shone through tree branches covered with Spanish moss. Shots fired in the distance. A girl, about nine or ten, talked about *Harry Potter.* Five women cooked biscuits and gravy over a Confederate campfire. Artillery members checked their cannons for 9:00 a.m. Colors at the thirty-ninth annual Brooksville Raid Reenactment. Lieutenant Colonel Keith Kohl addressed his Florida unit of the Confederate States.

"Three-fourths," he shouted. "Front, right!"

On that January morning, I had stood on the back of a John Deere Gator, which is a vehicle, not an animal. A former St. Petersburg police officer had driven me through the reenactor campground to Kohl's camp. Nearly 1,500 all-volunteer reenactors planned to take part in the weekend's events. They had already transformed the 1,300-acre Sand Hill Scout Reserve into an 1860s tent city. They constructed a big tent to accommodate Lady's tea and the reenactors-only ball on Saturday night as well as a Sunday-morning chapel service. Trees separated Confederate camp from Union camp, and more trees separated them from the civilian town. Rows of about fifty sutlers, the period vendors, sold items. People could buy wreaths made of Confederate flags, gowns, wood guns, $1,200 muskets, battle flags, candles "made by an old man in Virginia," time-period jewelry, knives, and dresses little boys would have worn until the age of about seven back in the 1800s.

The former police officer had stayed silent as he maneuvered past "modern camp" with RVs and other creature comforts. I tried to get him to talk to me, but he answered with skeptical grunts. He seemed relieved when I jumped off the Gator at Kohl's Confederate unit in "authentic camp," laid out according to U.S. Army Regs–1861. Gas stoves, lights, and radios were forbidden or at least had to be hidden from the public's view. Kohl and other authentic campers portrayed either real people who'd fought in the Civil War or a time-period persona they created. They remained in character for the whole weekend and gave first-person impressions to the expected nine thousand spectators who could stroll through their camps between battles.

The country's original Civil War reenactors descended from the war's soldiers. In the 1950s, these children or grandchildren began to give talks at schools in Chicago, Philadelphia, and Virginia. People saw them, thought, *wow, that's cool*, and joined their ranks. They stepped up their production value and staged battle reenactments for the centennial. The hobby gained popularity during the nineties, when *Glory* and *Gettysburg* reshaped the public's interest in the Civil War. Around 40 million Americans tuned into PBS to watch the eleven-hour Ken Burns miniseries on the subject. Those productions drew criticism for historical inaccuracies, but some reenactors told me their focus on the heroic and romantic aspect of soldiers' lives changed opinions on the war. The hobby has since experienced a decline in participation. Some younger recruits have lacked the same enthusiasm, the same buy-in. There's competition from technology, and many people question if these events should continue because of the country's ongoing racial tension.

Media depictions of reenactors ranged from a storyline in *Sweet Home Alabama* to a History Channel documentary. The term "Civil War reenactor," for some, had become shorthand for white, southern racist. I had never met an out-and-proud Civil War reenactor. I only knew them from these images as hillbilly cosplayers. I would have never gone to a Civil War reenactment if I hadn't wanted to write about Florida's place in "the South." These events made me uncomfortable; they seemed to celebrate a dark part of America's past. I understood the importance or value of re-creating history, but I didn't understand reenactments that people thought could perpetuate racist attitudes and behavior. To me, these reenactors embodied ugly parts of Florida's past and present.

Lieutenant Keith Kohl wore a gray shell jacket with a light-blue collar and gold adornments. His uniform included a sword, sword belt, revolver, canteen, and haversack. The whole outfit set him back about $750. This could be an expensive hobby, so he often lent loaner gear to newbies.

Keith had moved from his native Maryland at eleven years old. He saw his first Civil War reenactment near Gainesville in 1983. He reenacted three months later. The self-taught historian and author of *Florida's Civil War Years* had participated in the Brooksville Raid for about thirty-six years. "We're kind of like an extended family here," he said. Keith lived with his biological family near Ocala. His young son had already begun to reenact, but the toddler had stayed home for this raid. Keith camped out with his unit of about thirty-five members split between two battle companies.

Keith's unit consisted mostly of men, but one teenage girl stood among them. Women could reenact in combat, but their stipulations varied from event to event. I didn't think I'd encounter any drag kings at the reenactment, but Keith called it the ten-foot rule or the ten-yard rule. "At that distance, they must be indistinguishable as a woman," he said. "They have to pass as a guy." Their hair went up in a hat. If they were, Keith said, "putting it politely: well-endowed," they wore a loose-fitting jacket.

The lone girl in Keith's group had recently passed her driver's license test. This meant she was at least sixteen, the required age to shoot a gun in a reenactment battle. I watched the soldiers check to make sure only powder filled their time-period weapons. They made sure nothing dangerous hid in their guns. "All we do is pour black powder down the barrel," said Keith. Other weaponry guidelines included: No flintlock rifles allowed on the field. Shotguns or musketoons were only used with approval from the artillery commander. They couldn't ram cartridges with paper, and bayonets had to remain in scabbards.

"Want a uniform, buddy?" one of Keith's soldiers shouted to me from the line.

As the only man not in gear, I stood out from the crowd.

I had considered dressing out with reenactors from one of the Florida companies to get a more insider-y point of view. Prior experience wasn't required to reenact. Spectators got recruited. ("Momma, where is Daddy going?" I heard a little girl ask her mother. "He's off to war," her mother responded.) A commanding officer from a Florida Confederate unit cleared me to join them. One of the corporals asked me to send him my boot, shirt, pant, and head size. I sent them all but my head size because I didn't know how to measure my head. The corporal asked me if I'd want to shoot a cannon, and I, oddly, found this request appealing. I'd only shot a gun a few times in my life, mostly hunting with my grandfather. *If I really want to get into the culture*, I thought, *then I might as well shoot a cannon.* "We'll see," I said to the corporal.

A few days later I began to question if it would be a good idea for me to do Confederate cosplay, even if it was for a story. I talked about this with a colleague, and she brought up a different concern. She didn't know how kindly the reenactors, whom we assumed to be mostly conservative, would take to a gay dude. I started to feel like I should back out of the story, but I didn't want to tell only the pretty parts of Florida. I talked with my friend Jessica about the idea to dress as a Confederate, and she quickly killed the idea. "Don't do it," she said. "Someone will take a picture of you in the uniform, and it could go on the internet. People will think you're a racist." Jessica told me she didn't think reenacting was racist but that the Confederate flag was. I didn't understand how one could be racist and not the other, but it reminded me of a conversation we'd had years earlier. On a muggy night in Florida, we sat on front steps and talked to a woman with a Confederate flag tattoo on her shoulder. The tattoo shocked me, because it's like, *there it is, the Confederate flag on your body forever.*

"I'm sure you've seen my tattoo," the woman had said. "Do you think it makes me a racist?"

"Yes," said Jessica.

"Well, I'm not," the woman said, "and my family didn't own any slaves. I've done my research."

The woman and I had talked about family and the ways their stories shaped us. Her family had lived in my Florida hometown for generations, and she called herself a Cracker. She defended her tattoo. She said, *it represents how hard my family worked* and *the Civil War was about taxation and people need to do their research.*

I had done research since then, and I still didn't feel comfortable with the Confederate flag. The NAACP considered this flag a symbol that "glorified treason and a hateful history of white supremacy and black subjugation." In 2015, a couple thousand people rallied in central Florida to keep a Confederate flag displayed outside a government building. Protestors wore shirts with "heritage" printed next to the flag. The second-largest Confederate flag in the world had flown over a nearby interstate. My grandfather, born in Pennsylvania, had worn a Confederate flag belt buckle while my Floridian grandmother thought people should take down their Confederate flags.

Union commander Chuck Munson said, "If you're a Union reenactor there's not an issue at all, but if you're a Confederate reenactor, you could literally lose your job." Munson estimated over 95 percent of the Confederate reenactors wanted to honor their ancestors or were born in the North. "You've probably got less than 5 percent who are still fighting the war," he said, "and the rest are taking it on the chin. They're being politically attacked because somebody thinks they're still at fault for slavery."

Criticism of Civil War reenactments ramped up after Donald Trump became president. The 2017 "Unite the Right" rally in Charlottesville, Virginia, brought out white supremacist groups. They violently protested a plan to take down the city's monument of Confederate General Robert E. Lee. During the rally, neo-Nazis waved Confederate flags in front of the monument. A man dressed as a Civil War soldier saluted it. This rally changed the way some southerners, like the popular "Liberal Redneck" comedian Trae Crowder, saw the flag. "At this point there's no redeeming it," he told a Florida publication in 2019. "It means exactly what most people say it means: that you're intolerant at best and downright hateful and dangerous at worst." In the months after "Unite the Right," reenactment events received threats of violence. The FBI found an explosive device located on the grounds of a Civil War reenactment about an hour from Charlottesville. The town canceled the event. Illinois's Lake County Forest Preserves did, too. They cited public safety concerns.

Union reenactor Jacob McLaughlin told me the divisive political climate worried everybody. "I certainly keep that in mind when I'm out there," he said. "I know the people that are coming to watch this are also all caught up in what's going on, and I don't want the people to walk away feeling like one ideology or another is being pushed on them. I don't want people walking away feeling offended."

Several reenactors told me they focused less on the reasons for the war and more on their ancestors who fought in it. "Back then, they believed your state was your country," said Jeff Hardy, who had reenacted as a Florida Confederate for thirty-eight years. "They were defending their country." Jeff became involved in reenactment because he's a history buff. "All my ancestors fought for the Confederacy," he said. "None of them owned slaves. They were farmers."

We never owned slaves became a common refrain for many reenactors I interviewed. These reenactors, like the woman with the Confederate tattoo, may have fully believed their families didn't own enslaved people. These folks might have also extensively researched their family's wills and letters to find out this information. I took them at their word on heritage. I didn't point out historians argue that far more small farmers engaged in slave-owning practices than people know or care to admit, and, as Tracy Revels writes, "even if most individuals in Florida did not personally own slaves, slavery was part of the everyday experience in a third of Florida's white households [in the 1860s]." The reenactors' phrase *we never owned slaves* seemed to allow distance from the atrocities of the time.

I ultimately didn't dress up as a Confederate soldier. I didn't know if the uniform was inherently racist or not, but it didn't feel right for me. I still couldn't shake the thought that just because I didn't dress up like a Confederate soldier didn't mean I wouldn't have been one as a Floridian during the War.

I told Keith and the rest of his soldiers I'd watch them do their thing. No one seemed to care. They didn't pay attention to my internal conflict and existential crisis of heritage. They were too busy getting ready to fight.

Normally, the reenactors performed one battle for about an hour and fifteen minutes. For this day, they planned battle scenarios spaced from noon to about 3:30. Soon, a chorus of shouts broke out as other commanders assembled.

"Sir, First Battalion, Department of the Gulf, all present and accounted for, sir."

"Sir, Southern Volunteers, all present and accounted for, sir."

"Sir, Second Florida Cavalry, all present and accounted for, sir."

"Battalion," a commander said, "attention to arms. This parade is dismissed."

Spectators lined the field to watch. A soldier played "To Arms in Dixie" on a fife. Keith marched his unit into the woods.

More than 15,000 Floridians fought for the Confederacy while another 1,200 white Floridians served in Union forces along with about 1,000 freed slaves and free black Floridians. In 1864, the Union stormed Brooksville. They wanted to stop the area from channeling goods to the Confederates. The Union encountered old men, young boys, and a few women who could shoot. These scrappy townspeople couldn't hold the line. The Union broke through the defense and "cut a swath of destruction." They took Brooksville's cattle and cotton.

Florida saw few major battles because of the state's geographical location and undeveloped land. One major battle occurred in north Florida at the Pond of Olustee, which gets commemorated with a reenactment like Brooksville's. Florida supplied the Confederacy with thousands of heads of cattle. And Olustee had beef. The Union wanted to "interdict the flow of cattle into Georgia." Florida cattle was the state's main contribution to the war and kept many soldiers fed. The Confederacy won at Olustee. A member of the Union infantry described the Union's defeat as "a failure; in other words, our troops ha[d] been badly whipped."

Most of the state's soldiers fought outside of Florida. Confederate Florida soldier William McLeod kept a Civil War diary of his time in the Seventh Regiment. Born in South Carolina, McLeod moved to Florida near the age of five. He enlisted in the war from Manatee County. His regiment fought battles in Chattanooga, Atlanta, and in the Carolinas Campaign. McLeod documented marches, of 3 to 20 miles a day, and the injured, "3 of our men were wounded & the Capt & 3 men surrendered & 2 come out unhurt." He tallied captured prisoners, "negroes 700 & whites 300" and described times he was "lying in the ditches waiting the movement of the enemy and God only knows what tomorrow may bring forth."

Students heard stories like McLeod's during the Brooksville Raid's school day, a field trip held the Friday before the reenactment. Reenactors answered questions during living histories. They discussed why their personas fought for the cause. Organizers approved me to attend the school day, but they denied my access when I checked in on Friday. They said I would have needed school clearance for me to attend the event. I'm not going to speculate on their reasons for not letting me know this sooner.

Union reenactor Chuck Munson told me an estimated two thousand students crammed into buses to hear him and other Living Historians. Chuck described the "glow" of one of these students. "I reached out and I brought history alive to him," he said. "The good feeling of seeing the history come alive, the adrenaline rush, was phenomenal." The semi-native Floridian talked to the school day students about the war's realities for the common man. "I mean, I like going out and playing army," he said, "but the most important part of this hobby for me is sharing the knowledge I've gained with years of research."

Jacob McLaughlin said the living history aspect had drawn him to the hobby as well. He served in the Marine Corps and found work as a park ranger for the National Park Service in Glacier Bay, Alaska. He believed "in social change and feels that this period in history holds many examples." He reenacted because he thought history should be a springboard for modern conversations. "This history has to be remembered," he said, "and it has to be presented in such a way that people understand what the consequences of this sort of division could be."

The thirty-seven-year-old grew up about an hour north of Orlando. He didn't consider himself a full-blown southerner because his father transplanted from New York City. Jacob was soft-spoken and thoughtful. I got the poet-vibe from him. He described himself as northern stock raised in a southern environment. His hometown was very conservative, very religious, and very rural. He had found a surprising diversity in reenactors' political beliefs and backgrounds. "I wouldn't want to see this go away," he said. "I would hope the generation coming up would see the importance of continuing with this tradition regardless of where they fall on the political spectrum."

Jacob said these events gave him a unique way to present an important part of history. "We see what happened in our history, and even though slavery was abolished, and the outcome was positive, the problems didn't go away," he said. "Our differences remained. We're still dealing with the war's effects, and nobody out here wants to see that history repeated."

At first, the cannons jolted me, but I grew somewhat accustomed to them. Articles about reenactors described them as old men with white beards and round bellies. These descriptions proved accurate for some but not all of the reenactors. As the battle raged for over an hour, I noticed a fifteen-year-old boy in Keith's unit.

Blake Cooper loaded his rifle. A boy who looked to be about eleven or twelve stood to his right. Child soldiers were common in the war. An estimated 10 to 20 percent of the three-million-plus soldiers were under eighteen when they signed up to fight. I watched as the Union charged over a hill toward the young soldiers. Horses pulled a small cannon. "The ones in the Blue are us," someone near me said. There were more cannon blasts. Men fell to the ground as a boy too young for combat helped others with ammunition.

Keith commanded his line to move, and three men died at the same time. Blake easily cleared six feet tall, but he still had a baby face. He wore a canteen and drank from it as his line moved closer to the crowd. In a flash, he hunched over. He'd been shot. He fell and stood back up. Confederate soldiers laid flat around him. Another teen kneeled with a bloody bandage wrapped around his head.

The action quieted.

A Union soldier played taps. Spectators picked up their blankets and headed toward their cars. Dead soldiers from both sides rose like zombies. The reenactors formed a line in front of those who remained. They raised their rifles to the sky and shifted their stances. On orders, they fired.

Genie Stracuzzi watched these final gunshots from the civilian town at the back end of the battlefield. During the war, civilians had tried to continue their daily routines as best they could. Civilian life sometimes got overlooked in reenactments, so Genie and other authentic reenactors—sometimes called progressive—created the Florida Authentic Civilian Town (FACT). Civil War soldiers came out of farms, factories, law offices, and doctor's offices. They vacated those positions, and women stepped in to continue the businesses. FACT's current town employed a laundress and a postmistress who took over her husband's job.

Civilian reenactors ate meals and washed clothes as soldiers fought. Some of them spun wool or knitted. Information traveled slowly during the war. Those who stayed behind heard rumors and talk. Some wrote letters to find out how nearby townspeople fared and if they had survived. "There are so many different avenues with the civilian aspect," said Genie. "My goal is to educate the public on what civilians went through during this time." FACT's townspeople didn't get involved in the politics, and they didn't fly any kind of battle flags. "We try to be neutral," she said. "It's an education process."

I couldn't help but like Genie. I admired her historical accuracy. I had worried the reenactors wouldn't want to talk to me, but she made me feel comfortable. The fifty-eight-year-old discovered reenactment as a history event for her homeschooled children. The seventh-generation Floridian reenacted in the state, and she traveled across the country to events with her "Yankee" husband. "I know," she said. "My daddy is going, what in the world were you thinkin'? A Yankee Italian out of New York, but he was a sweetheart." Her Yankee Italian didn't attend the Brooksville Raid because of a nasty cough. "He loves to do this," she said, "just don't ask him to put a southern twang in his voice because it doesn't work." The couple averaged about one reenactment per month. They attended national events with a lot of authentic guidelines they had to emulate.

Genie conducted genealogical research to find her main persona, her "great-, great-, great-grandmother" Mary. "I was able to research what my family did for a living," she said. Genie preferred to reenact as Mary, but she only portrayed this family member when the reenactment took place in a Florida setting. The weekend's reenactment included several battles at different locations. When we talked, it was a town in Virginia. She and other FACT townspeople pulled the town's census records from 1860, but they ran into a problem. The census had burned in battle. The FACT women had to look one county over for census records to create personas.

Genie wore a faded purplish-gray dress with what she called a working cage or working hoop. It was shorter and smaller than the hoop women wore to balls. FACT townspeople weren't supposed to wear fine silks during the battle. Genie brought a dress for the night's ball. "That's my dress cage," she said, pointing to a garment hung near her bed. "If you go visiting with your neighbors or to a tea or a dance then you would wear that." Genie tried to keep-it-1860 as much as possible, from dishes to the food put on those dishes. She wasn't allowed to have any bananas because in 1864 there was no way to have fresh bananas delivered to Petersburg, Virginia. Instead of fresh fruits, she ate "mostly hard cheeses."

The FACT townspeople maintained their guidelines, but Genie begrudgingly bent them a little. The town had to use tents instead of constructing historically accurate houses. "We can't build a home in four days," she said, "so we chose to live in these tents, and we pretend that they're houses."

Before I left her tent-house, Genie invited me to the reenactors-only ball. "It is such a hoot," she said. "That's where you learn the period dances. It's so much fun." She and the other FACT reenactors didn't plan to attend the ball, though. She leaned in close to me and whispered there was going to be an evening raid. "I hope that nobody comes through during our meal and forages us," she said. "At about 6:30 this evening. Just so you know."

I planned to visit Genie during her 6:30 raid, but nightfall made the campsites difficult to navigate. Fires lit paths. The camps didn't use modern lights. I had felt somewhat comfortable roaming the grounds during the day, but things changed in the moonlight. I wondered about the tone of conversations held underneath the eerie trees. The reenactors I interviewed said they participated in the event for family and history. But I only saw what I saw and heard what I heard. No one had told me anything like *the South will rise again* or *slavery wasn't so bad*, but I didn't know what was said around these late-night campfires. I couldn't be sure what I would have heard or how the day would have gone if I wasn't a white guy.

In the darkness, I spotted the big, well-lit tent for the reenactors-only Blue Gray Ball. I found a seat in the tent and watched as people slowly filed into the striped structure. A woman walked in wearing an emerald dress with opaque gloves and a flower crown. Reenactors bought ball gowns and other costume pieces from sutlers. Vendors set up shop right outside the battlefield. Married couple Travis and April Stevens ran one of them called Possum Holler Sutlery. They sold a purple dress, handmade by Travis's mother. They traveled with their business from West Virginia to Texas to Alabama and back. Other sutlers stocked up on jewelry and battlefield gear. A man's jacket cost $122.50, and a musket went for around $1,000. Civilians didn't carry weapons to the night's event, which, the authentic reenactor Genie had said didn't technically constitute a ball. She called it a dance. A ball would have been held in a concrete or wooden building with calling cards, not on grass in a tent.

People partnered arm-in-arm as music began to play. They divided into groups to dance the Virginia reel. The youngest couple in the group nearest me were teenagers; the oldest looked to be somewhere in their sixties or seventies. "When you come forward to me," the dance caller said into a microphone, "you will bow or curtsy to me, and I will reciprocate. Then, I'll have you go either left or to the right. You know the routine."

The dancers clapped their hands and turned circles. Everyone laughed as couples skipped down the line. It looked like a fast-paced line dance.

Blake Cooper, the fifteen-year-old Confederate reenactor I spotted earlier in the battle, sat alone. He seemed tired. "My whole unit was destroyed today," he said. "I got shot three times, but I got up like I'm immortal." Cooper had first seen a reenactment five years earlier. He had then found a reenactment group online. He tried to get friends to join him with no luck. Blake estimated he'd been to at least thirty reenactments, and he hoped to one day teach history. The teenager wouldn't dance with a partner, but he did circle up for the "Drunken Sailor" dance. A group of about thirty guys formed a mosh pit. They jumped into each other during the Irish song about, as the title suggests, a drunk sailor. The quiet Blake, described as a "big teddy bear" by another reenactor, flung his body into the group with reckless abandon.

My eyes turned to a few other teens in the corner. They took a picture and held up what may or may not have constituted the "okay" hand signal. Far-right trolls adopted a similar sign. I couldn't be sure of the teens' intentions. As I figured out the best way to ask them, *hey, are y'all white supremacists?* they left the tent. The moment happened as quickly as their picture. It made me uncomfortable. (Union reenactor Jacob McLaughlin later told me that he and his camp "would be horrified to see teenagers making racist overtures at these events." His group kept a zero-tolerance policy for such behavior. "I'm sure there are those who harbor racist views or support neo-Confederate causes," he said, "but there are those of us who wish to honor those who fought against one of the greatest atrocities ever committed against humanity.") The day had worn me out, and I felt like I should leave.

Genie tapped me on the shoulder. She'd changed out of her earlier dress into a more ball-worthy gown. "The soldiers raided our dinner earlier," she said. "It was awesome." She introduced me to other FACT reenactors who'd come out to the ball. "I told Tyler he had to dance," she said to them. "Whatever happens in the tent, stays in the tent."

I didn't necessarily enjoy dancing with a partner with all those steps and awkward small talk. My dance style was more of a flail my arms, do a spin, and a jump kick if I'm feelin' it kind of thing.

"This is a free dance," Genie said. "Basically, it's a polka. A two-step."

Men clapped their hands, and women adjusted their hoop skirts. Couples danced all around us. I smiled at Genie. We started our two-step under the tent. The music sped up, and we did, too.

The following morning H. K. Edgerton stood in front of Keith's Confederate unit. H. K. was one of two black Confederate reenactors I saw during the weekend. The unit had chosen him to lead the day's battalion. The seventy-one-year-old with salt-and-pepper hair wore a gray shell jacket. He gripped a large Confederate flag, at least half his body size.

H. K. didn't reenact much anymore, but he had traveled to Florida for the raid's schoolday. He planned to attend the next day's MLK parade. He would then celebrate the sixteenth anniversary of his walk to Texas in a Confederate uniform. "The Confederate flag is a venerated symbol from the United States Congress," he said. "The laws should be applied equally, but they don't apply to southern folks. We should not be told to take our flag down and go home."

I wanted to ask him how he felt to be a black reenactor surrounded by so many white faces. I wanted to know if he felt tokenized. I tried to formulate a thoughtful question, but I became hesitant.

"Why is it important for you to represent what you're doing?" I asked.

"I wish you would have gone on and said to represent the black Confederate soldiers," he said. "Because as we approach Black History Month, the public-school system will not be talking about them."

African Americans fought for both sides in the war. Historians debate the word "soldier" for the Confederacy. John Coski wrote that tens of thousands of enslaved and free African Americans served with Confederate armies as body servants, laborers, teamsters, hospital workers, and cooks. These laborers weren't formally enlisted or compensated for their work. Some free African Americans pledged themselves to the Confederacy. Some also owned enslaved people. Professor John Stauffer wrote the show of support for the Confederacy made them "race traitors."

H. K. gave me his thoughts on the "traitor status." He told me the black men who fought for the Confederacy deserved respect because they helped build the country. He thought the Confederate flag represented them. "People want to destroy the Confederates' legacy and lives," he said. "They want to talk about them as rednecks, but they were farmers and successful men who believed in states' rights." H. K.'s affiliations with southern heritage groups made him a controversial figure. He "rebuffed" both the NAACP and Black Lives Matter movement. People have said he's fighting the good fight while others have called him an Uncle Tom. "Let me tell you, I get about 98 percent love," he said, "but I did get my teeth knocked out at a Veteran's Day parade."

He and I stood together in a camp right off the battlefield. I wanted to ask him more about the work he dedicated his life to doing. I wanted more than his rehearsed answers, but I couldn't get them out of him. And people kept interrupting us. They wanted a picture with him and all the medals on his jacket.

H. K. led Keith and the other Confederate reenactors onto the battlefield. It had rained the previous night, and the crowd dwindled as more rain threatened. Cannons fired from the far end of the field, and Union soldiers charged as they had the previous day.

As I watched the final battle of the Brooksville reenactment, I thought about Florida's past and how to remember it—both the good and the bad. Southerners, even the Florida variety, must grapple with their history and identity. They must do this as some people call the South stupid and backward. Criticism of reenactors extended past their hobby to conversations on the possibility for the South to reconcile its symbols and heritage. This conversation should be a national one about our country's history, but it often fell on the South's shoulders.

The reenactment began to wind down, and Tiffany Davis walked up to me. "Have you collected enough information?" she asked. "I saw you the other day in my authentic camp." Tiffany had spent her first full reenactment with Keith and other soldiers in his unit. Throughout the weekend, she had helped keep the campsite running. Tiffany said she'd caught the reenacting bug. "It is quite a reality check between modern-day living and how they actually lived," she said. "It's fascinating and frightening how anyone ever lived through it."

The native Floridian hadn't felt strongly about being a "Confederate lady" over a "Union lady." Her friend reenacted as a Confederate, so she decided to as well. Her real-life brother portrayed a Union soldier, which made for interesting dinner conversation. "I'm learning a lot about Civil War history," she said. "You kind of feel transported back in time when you reenact, and that was the most fascinating part. I felt connected to the people who actually lived here back then."

Across from us, two young boys stood with their father. I watched as reenactors staggered on the field and dropped to the ground. Gunsmoke enveloped them. An evening wind blew, chilly from the night's rain. The boys huddled together, and their father wrapped them in a rebel flag for warmth.

LANDSCAPE
WITH CRACKERS

A group of cows appeared like a mirage near my apartment in Orlando, a city full of traffic and tourists. The large animals seemed so idiosyncratic and surreal. They grazed with snowy egrets behind a barbed-wire fence. I had moved to Orlando for a teaching job, and the cows stared at me on my commute. I began to notice them more and more. The cows were like blue cars on the highway after someone told you to look for them.

Cows had lived in Florida for centuries. Nine of the nation's top-twenty-five cow-calf operations called the state home. After I noticed the cows near my apartment, I spotted others eating in pastures; they did this on just over 15 percent of the state's land. I wanted to find out more about these Florida cows, so I met sixth-generation Florida cowman Cary Lightsey. He co-owned ranches with his brother in central Florida's Lake Wales. "We've got eight generations of ranchers here," said Cary. "This is what we like to do, but some days I don't know why we like it."

By midmorning, Cary had already shot a coyote and a pair of wild hogs that tried to kill a baby calf. "One of the worst things for our land is the hogs," he said. "You can't shoot them all, but I wish you could." Spaniards brought the invasive hogs to the U.S. mainland in the 1500s. Anywhere from 500,000 to a million of them wandered the Sunshine State in 2018. Male hogs averaged about 200-plus pounds and reached almost 5 feet in length. They horrified me and made my top-ten list of scary animals (coming in behind hippos and before wolves). These hogs weren't cute like Piglet from *Winnie the*

Pooh. They were more like the *Lord of the Flies* pig-head on a stick, which the internet told me was a symbol for the devil. The hogs got freaking huge and mean. Sows could produce two litters a year, and, if nutrition was poor, they ate their young. I'm not trying to shame the hogs—it's not their fault they're in Florida—but they caused a lot of problems. They could tear up a plot in minutes. An early Floridian documented the "roving hogs" that rooted her "potatoes as none but a Florida hog can." "Last year," she wrote in 1883, "the hogs took everything." Feral hogs hunted alone or in packs. They ate with a teenage boy's appetite—anything from acorns to grass to grasshoppers, fish, fawns, and livestock. "I don't hunt," said Cary, "but I can't handle the hogs killing our babies."

Cary wore a long-sleeved checkered shirt, a silver star belt buckle, and a white ten-gallon hat. The sixty-seven-year-old did three hundred sit-ups in the mornings. He ate a steak just about every day. This routine almost put him back to his fighting weight after a ranch accident nearly killed him.

Three years earlier, the cowman set out to rope an aggressive heifer, or, as he called her, a "hairy Mary." He'd done this kind of work since childhood. His father worked as a rancher as did his grandfather and generations of men in their family before them. Cary had mounted his horse. The hairy Mary wasn't fond of his pursuit. She stuck a big horn in the horse's rear quarter. Cary rode the heifer down until his head snapped back. He went unconscious. He awoke to his crew roping the heifer off him. "I had so many broken bones, you could hear them grinding," he said. "I thought I was dying." Cary had broken his collarbone, shoulder, ribs, leg, and tailbone. He severed the artery going into his kidney. Punctured a lung. Pulled an Achilles.

Marcia, his wife of nearly forty-six years, saw the whole thing. The couple met in high school, and she worked on the ranch with him ever since their postgraduation nuptials. "I've pulled Cary out of the woods many a times from his horse falling on him," she said, "but this accident was traumatizing."

Cary woke up in a hospital room surrounded by about twenty-five family members. They were crying. He thought he'd gone to heaven, and his family couldn't see him. The real-life, breathing doctor gave him a diagnosis of, *the good news is you're going to live, but the bad news is there's an 8-pound tumor near your liver.* He had been born with the tumor, but this was the first he'd ever heard of it. Previous doctors diagnosed the lump in his belly as arthritis. "One more month and the tumor would have been in my liver," he said. "If I wouldn't have had the accident, I wouldn't be here." Cary thanked God for his recovery. He'd always been a religious man, the kind of person who listened to Christian radio and prayed before meals.

He recovered and continued to work on the ranch. His family owned around 18,000 acres. (I don't recommend you ask a cowboy how much land or cattle he owns because, as I was told later, those two questions are usually off-limits.) I climbed into his blue F250 with a front plate that read: *Go Gators! Enjoy more Beef.* He took me to where he runs cattle. He and ten other cowboys drove about 380 cows over five miles. The cattle would start off spunky and then get tired. They'd stop and rest in the shade before being branded and sorted. Ranchers spend countless hours with their livestock. It takes about two years for cattle to make weight before they reach a restaurant plate. I don't want to upset vegans more than I already have, but the hides of those restaurant cows can also be used in by-products like athletic equipment, makeup, glue; their hair for air filters, artist brushes, upholstery stuffing; their blood for anti-inflammation treatments.

Cary's wife, Marcia, struggled with the cow life cycle when she first moved to the ranch. Marcia, the nicest person anyone could ever want to talk to, didn't grow up on a ranch. She never thought she'd marry a cowboy. She grew up in a military family. And while by no means a city girl, Marcia wasn't used to the cowboy life. She fell in love with the cows and wanted to name them. Marcia saw the cows as extended family members. She'd bottle-raise them and took it to heart when one died of a lightning strike or drowned in a ditch. She couldn't bear it when they had to ship the cows off to market.

She had to harden herself. She got to the point where she couldn't look at cows as her favorite anymore. "We care for them, but things are going to happen," she said. "I finally had to just tell myself, don't get special because when it's time for them to leave—or they die in the pasture—I can't have such an emotional tie to the cow." Marcia stopped treating them special, but she still got excited about calf season. She still oohed over the calves and thought, *oh, that one would be cute for the state fair next year.*

Marcia learned the bookkeeping side from Cary's mom and the

physical work of ranch life from Cary. She began to tend cattle and broke one bone in her forty-six years of cow work. That day, she'd been counting cattle when one of the heifers pinned her wrist to the gate. She went back to work in a couple of weeks. Marcia worked with the nonprofit organization Florida Cattlewomen, which was formed to help promote the cattle industry and educate the public. She was named the 2003 Florida Outstanding Cattlewoman of the Year. "So many people think we do everything mechanically," she said, "that there's no concern or passion."

These ranchers dealt with the emotions, habits, and moods of large animals. "We want our cows happy because happy cows mean happy ranchers," said Marcia. "We don't want to misuse or abuse our cattle." Each Lightsey family member, except their three-year-old grandchild, played a role on the ranch. One of the Lightsey's three children lived next door to Cary and Marcia. Another lived down the shell road with six children of his own, and a third lived on one of the family's other ranches.

Cary introduced me to some of his family's cattle. They were all different colors: white, black, brown, reddish, and in between. Different breeds had different smells and abilities. He said black cows liked the shade. White cows didn't mind the temperature as much. The cows in Cary's pasture stared at me. They looked surprised but resolute, like *you make the first move, buddy*. Cary said they knew him but not me. I put them on edge. Cows, like middle school kids, didn't want to invite the new guy to sit with them.

Cary's cows ate a dessert-lover's fever dream; their feed was a mix of Publix donuts, cakes, cookies, pastries, and bread. The grocery chain couldn't sell the products after a certain date. They also couldn't take them to a landfill because of their methane gas emission. The store delivered its old baked goods to the ranch. A machine then sucked the package off the pastries, which were ground and heated. This process also happened with produce from Walmart and grain from Budweiser. It took about six hours to go from truck to grinder to sugary mix. The ranch's machinery had transformed, but the cowboys still used a horse and dogs and popped a whip to get the cows moving.

Cary took me to a pasture he called the hospital. One of his heifers could produce calves for about fourteen to eighteen years. After that, arthritis set in as it had with Cary's own bones. Aging cows retired and received extra care like a nursing home before they went to the great McDonald's in the sky. "The main thing we want to do is to make our cows fat," he said. "It won't make you any money unless it's fat. You got to work at it, and the people who don't want to work at it, don't stay in the business."

Cattle, like much of Florida, dates to the Spanish conquistadors of the early 1500s La Florida. Apparently, Ponce de León wanted to eat a burger. He put cows on ships and brought beef to the peninsula. The indigenous people shot arrows at Ponce to protect their land. He turned around and got back on his ship and left the cattle to freely roam. The Spaniards came back to La Florida and bred the cattle. By 1700, around 1,620 head of cattle lived on the land (compared to about 1.68 million head in 2019). Florida became a U.S. territory in 1821 and a slave state in 1845. Cattle proved Florida's major contribution to the Civil War, and some of the Lightsey family's stock went to the Confederacy. He showed me a rusty-looking branding iron the members of his family may have used during the Civil War.

Early Floridian cattle ranchers were often known as "cowmen" or "cow hunters." They received this badass moniker because they tracked down free-roaming cattle in roundups. At times, cowman and Cracker have been used interchangeably. The term "Cracker" can make some folks uncomfortable. I had read it came from a cowboy's whip-crack. I had also read the term originated from "the white slave driver." As it turns out, neither of those origins proved altogether true. The Scots-Irish brought the term with them to North America. By the late 1700s, a Cracker was basically a rascal or a good-for-nothing. The term went on to mean different things in different mouths. But in the United States, Cracker "has almost always been used disparagingly to describe the mudsills of the South."

Certain Floridians—like the Lightsey family and mine—didn't mind being called Crackers. My great-granny Lula used to take me to my hometown's annual "Cracker Supper." At this Cracker supper, a meal I referred to as "dinner," my granny talked to friends from high school. They wore cut-out oranges pinned as nametags. Their curled hair stuck in place by hairspray and hot weather. They gave me hugs and asked, "How's your momma?" Granny Lula talked to her friends, and I drank the best tasting OJ I've ever had. From the serving line,

I piled my plate with cornbread. The cooks brought out big, metal pots of collard greens. Other kids my age liked pizza or chicken nuggets, but my favorite food was collards. I drenched them in white vinegar. I ate the leafy greens until I felt sick. The term Cracker for my family and folks at the dinner linked us to Florida pioneers who had helped develop the state's land, culture, and economy.

Lightsey's kin had been one of those pioneering families. In 1712, his ancestors immigrated from Germany and settled in South Carolina. They stayed there for about eighty years and worked in the cattle business. The third generation took cattle to Georgia. They arrived in Florida sometime near 1837 and saw a land full of marshes and beautiful, green grass. They could buy property for "three or five or ten cents an acre." As a teenager, Cary learned to drive cattle on land his family had owned since the 1850s. He braved the elements and wore a slicker to lead cattle through thunderstorms. When a storm stopped, he saw four hundred heads of cattle and sun rays. He thought it one of the best things he'd ever seen. Cary's teenage ranch years prepared him to wrangle cattle, but they hadn't prepared him for the sudden loss of his father, who died when Cary was in his early twenties.

His father had not written a will. The family got hit with a high estate tax to the tune of nearly $1.3 million. They couldn't pay the bill and wondered if they should go get jobs at the power company. "We decided that's not an option," said Marcia. "We decided to tighten our belts." The couple moved into a trailer and sometimes ate the wild hogs that roamed central Florida. Cary started to sell them to a hunting reserve in Tennessee for fifty dollars apiece.

Their hog-trapping hustle of the 1980s paved the way for the Lightsey brothers' hog hunts. They took people out to search for hogs on the family's small island located in Lake Kissimmee. One day, a news anchor hunted a boar on assignment. "He shot a boar and showed it on TV," said Cary. This TV segment helped garner their initial hunting groups. Before they knew it, they were leading hunts for a couple hundred people. It became a moneymaker. The quality of their hunting ground attracted celebrities, some of whom didn't want the public to know they liked to hunt. Cary promised those secret hunters he wouldn't tell on them. One celebrity he could talk about was Shaquille O'Neal. The NBA superstar visited the Lightsey family almost every year. Cary could also tell me that someone

People magazine once named "Sexiest Man Alive" hunted hogs on the island. The Lightsey family led these hunts for more than thirty years, but they stopped to focus on their cattle business. They leased their hog-hunting land to four billionaires who were friends with Donald Trump. The president had, on occasion, flown the high-class hunters to the island. Cary said one reason the hogs had become such a big problem in Florida was because of a change in the state's laws. "Now, the laws say you can't move them over state lines," he said. "They lost their value, and something becomes a worse problem when there's no value to it."

The feral swine threatened his land, but he also contended with more aggressive animals: investors. "You've got two kinds of ranchers," said Cary, "the established ranchers—the pioneer people—and then you've got the investors." The website Farmflip.com helped these investors buy and sell farms. When I checked it, the site listed its most expensive farmland in Saint Lucie County for $97 million. Its cheapest listed in Suwanee County for $15,500. These investors, Cary said, often came to Florida from up North. They had made some money and wanted to put it in Florida land. They'd develop the land and then sell it for upward of triple the asking price. "They don't care about the future of our state," he said. "If we run out of resources, they'll just leave."

Investors hadn't always been so keen to drop money on land for Cracker cattle. After the Civil War, Florida cattle production declined because of the land's "nutritional deficiencies and tick fever." In the late 1890s, cattle went for ten dollars a head, and the selling price of herds cost even less at five dollars a head. Newspapers listed these prices as well as published cow poetry. One of my favorite cow poems, "An Agricultural Ode," contained the lines: "The beef steers sleek, plump and fat / To the butcher block must go / Before one pound of steak can be obtained / To quench the hungering of the inner man."

The "hungering of the inner man" drove the early cattle industry, but Florida's swampy terrain proved difficult to cultivate. A newspaper wrote the state had a vast quantity of unproductive land of little worth except for stock raising. "Even then," the paper continued, "it takes a hundred acres to keep a cow half starved." These half-starved cows roamed freely about the state. There weren't many fences or herders, and branding determined ownership. Resourceful Floridians came up with a solution. They advocated for proper fencing and the planting of more suitable grass.

Florida ranchers planted nutrient-rich grasses in the "improved pasture era" of the early twentieth century. They used fertilizer with phosphorous and nitrogen. Those nutrients occurred in nature and proved essential for plant growth, but their nutrient-runoff filtered into interconnected bodies of water.

Water issues became big news in 2018. I, like many other Florida journalists, worked on stories about red tide. The summer produced horrific images of beached whales, bloated dolphins, and distorted manatees. At one point, a reported 33 tons of dead fish had been collected from the beaches I had walked as a kid with Mom. The devastation looked apocalyptic. As I do when I'm upset about something, I started to write about it. I talked to experts and armchair experts. They blamed the state's water issues on a constellation of factors: pollen, global warming, Big Sugar, the Army Corps of Engineers, leaky septic tanks, the government, fertilizer, nutrient runoff from roadways, stormwater ponds, residential lawns, pollution, people's behavior, copper pesticides, and herbicides. No one seemed to know the exact cause.

To me, the most surprising alleged culprit was Florida's ranchers.

Biologist John Fauth worked with some of them. He told me central Florida ranches affected the water because of drainage and filtration. Chemicals in fertilizers flowed down to the Everglades and into the water. The extra nutrient runoff caused problems. The ranchers' improved pastures often harbored a legacy of phosphorous use. It was hard for a nutrient-enriched system to change back to its natural state. Florida ecologist Patrick Bohlen explained it as a buildup of nutrients in the soil. The buildup contributed phosphorus to the water pumps. Both John and Patrick talked about the conservation work of Florida ranchers. Overdevelopment proved the much bigger issue. "If Florida doesn't build smartly, it could get into the same boat as New Jersey," said John. "That state has squandered its natural resources. We have to pay a lot more attention."

Conservation-minded Florida ranchers like Cary Lightsey had moved away from phosphorous-heavy fertilizers. He took two samples a year ever since high school to make sure phosphorus levels on his land weren't too high. "Having clean land is important to me," he said. "I don't want to be blamed for anything." The Lightsey family helped pave the way for sustainable cattle ranching in the state. Audubon Florida recognized them as the "Sustainable Rancher of the Year" in 2016. The family placed over 90 percent of their land in conservation easements. These were agreements to prohibit residential or commercial development. Easements helped keep developments off land and agriculture on it.

The family worked their land with a rotating group of interns from the University of Florida and Warner University. The interns, Cary said, used to be mostly men, but recent cohorts had been mostly women. Mikayla Allison began as one of the Lightsey Cattle Company interns. The then Warner student drove cattle, gave them injections, sorted, tagged, and branded them. Mikayla described the Lightsey family as "selfless and compassionate about the environment." "They're good stewards of the land," she said. The Lightsey interns work this land alongside cowboys-for-hire. These were rugged cowboys—the type of guys who'd be perfect for a truck commercial.

The cowboys-for-hire went from ranch to ranch and got paid for their knowledge, dog, and rope. They kept no certain hours and usually worked until dark-thirty. Marcia stayed with the cow crew and helped cook cowboy meals like sausage and casserole for breakfast; a lunch of baked ham with homegrown peas and maybe a pecan pie or peach cobbler for dessert. "The guys are Florida Crackers," she said. "They all know what guava jelly is." The cowboys often gained weight from this home cooking. "They get home from working with us," said Marcia, "and they can't fit in their jeans." Marcia's food almost made me want to sign up to work as a cowboy-for-hire until I remembered the wild hogs and all the broken bones and who I generally am as a person.

Cary said his day-to-day job hadn't changed much over his four decades of work, but his clientele had. He found this out one day when a group of women stopped by his ranch. Cary and his crew were settling down some cattle when a car came bee-bopping through the double gates of his property. The little sedan got to them, and four women stepped out of the vehicle. The cows, as they had with me, didn't love the idea of new people in their midst. The cattle got a bit scared as the sedan's leader approached Cary. She told him, *we're here to buy a cow*. The group said they wanted to eat local beef. They wanted to know where the meat came from. Cary said, *OK, but ma'am it don't work that way*. He explained they couldn't just buy one of his cows and take it home to eat. They told him, *well, that's what we want to do*.

Cary relayed this story to a sustainability group. The group said that they, too, wanted the opportunity to visit a ranch and see the cows before they ate them. "I'm not what you call a high-tech computer guy," he said, "but I thought there might be something to it." He and a group of ranchers formed the Florida Cattle Ranchers (FCR). They focused on sustainable land practices and locally sourced cattle.

In general, Florida ranchers often shipped their cattle out of state to feed. The big feed yards didn't exist in Florida because it cost a lot to ship grain and corn, a staple ingredient in feed for a hundred years. Florida could grow a lot of things—like oranges and strawberries—but corn, not so much. Feed yards in states like Nebraska and Kansas could be humongous and feed about 50,000-plus head. Shipping cattle to a feed yard was like sending them to sleepaway camp. The Lightsey family had to trust the feed yards wouldn't hurt the cows. They would often visit their stock.

FCR created a Florida feed yard. This kept the cows closer to home. The homegrown feed yards weren't as big as those in the Midwest, so it took the cattle a little longer, about a year, to reach size. This proved more expensive, but FCR wanted their beef to stay in Florida. FCR members originally sold their beef to a grocery chain, but they decided to focus on food service and restaurants. The closest restaurant sold a burger named for the Lightsey family and made of their stock. Cary said he'd never seen anyone finish the double cheeseburger with bacon.

After we got done on the ranch, he took me to the nearby restaurant. I'm a meat-eater from way back. I often crave a big burger. Cary ordered a burger with no bun, and I chose the massive Lightsey burger. I wanted to see if I could be the first to finish it. Cary was a regular in the restaurant, as I would be anyplace with my name on the menu. Diners came over to chat with him and shake his hand. One of his former interns sat at a booth near us. Cary cracked jokes with the waitress when she brought our meal. He asked if he could say a prayer before we ate.

I bit into the burger and let its juices drip down my chin. The meat tasted delicious and fancy. Cary continued to talk to me about Marcia and his grandchildren, but I focused on the meat. I thought about all the work it took the Lightsey family and other ranchers to get this burger on my plate. I soon only had a few bites left. Cary told me he didn't think I'd be able to finish the burger, but I channeled my inner cowboy and ate every last every bite.

A couple of weeks later, I sat in a truck on a ranch in Wauchula, a Florida town somewhere near the middle of the state with a population of about five thousand. The area around this ranch looked a lot like other rural Florida cities I'd visited. They'd been a succession of fast-food chains, Walmart, and long strips of land. Doyle Carlton III, another FCR member, let his truck idle. He leaned over and said, "Oh, have I got a poaching story for you."

Doyle's family lived in Florida longer than anyone could remember. The seventy-one-year-old was a seventh-generation Floridian and the grandson of the state's twenty-fifth governor. His family settled on the land in the mid-1800s, and he worked with cattle about three days a week. He spent the other two days either in his office or doing board member work for the State Fair. "Ranching is all we know how to do," he said. "It's all we've ever done." Throughout our morning together, Doyle had been mostly reserved—a study in contrast to Cary. He'd become a bit more animated with the mention of poaching.

In the 1980s, Doyle's ranch grew clover eaten by both cattle and deer. One day, he noticed the property's deer unusually skittish. He suspected poachers. Sure enough, he was right. A worker he'd hired to harvest seed had organized a group to scour the property at night. They would kill the deer to sell their horns and meat. The ranch involved the game warden, who went undercover and got in with the crowd. The warden discovered these poachers listened to Doyle's crew talk on the porch at night. They'd wait until the lights went off. Then they'd hunt the deer and leave before the cowmen went out at sunrise. The warden wouldn't drop the net on the guys. He said, *just give us some time.*

The warden found out these poachers weren't just killing deer. They also grew marijuana on Doyle's property. And it wasn't just any marijuana. It was a popular and allegedly potent strain of weed (I never smoked it, so I'm unable to corroborate said potency). Authorities convicted several of Doyle's poachers-turned-pot-growers. A court sentenced the main pot guy to life in prison. (Doyle didn't want me to name anyone in this poaching/weed story because the guys were still alive. He didn't "want to do anything to hurt them personally.") The main pot guy served around ten years in prison before he received a presidential pardon.

Years after the bust, the pot guy's son—who'd also gone to prison for the operation—contacted Doyle. He'd found Jesus in prison and wanted to make restitution for some of the things he'd done. He asked Doyle if he could take him up the creek to show him where they had been growing the marijuana. Doyle declined. "I was thinking he just got out of prison and his daddy is still in prison," he said. "I ain't going up the creek with him." Doyle avoided him until a fateful Sunday. The pot guy's son showed up to church. Doyle taught a Sunday school class, and the son sat in on it. "We kind of had an ongoing relation after that," said Doyle, "but I haven't seen him in years."

Doyle's story was one of the reasons I loved Florida. It was a tale of two Florida men: one, the Christian cowboy kin to a governor, and the other, the son of a legendary pot-grower. In Florida, people never know who's going to end up a neighbor, so, as the good Lord says, Floridians should learn to love them all.

Doyle had lived among his more upstanding Wauchula neighbors his whole life. The area hadn't grown in the same ways as other parts of the state. "We kind of like it that way," he said. His two children worked for the ranch as well as his three grandsons. His granddaughter worked in the office, and his son-in-law worked for their citrus arm. Other family members helped with the business as well. A bunch of them lived in six or seven houses on the same street. "Ranching is what we love to do," he said. "We don't feel like daggum, I gotta be a cowboy."

Doyle loved his job and said he cared about the way people viewed his profession. His ranching industry's reputation had run the gamut. The public viewed them anywhere from the "white hat" conservationists to the "black hat land-rapers." In 2017, a disturbing "undercover video" came out of Larson Dairy in Okeechobee, Florida. The video showed several dairy workers kicking and punching cows. It was tough to watch. The video produced by a Miami-based "animal cruelty investigative organization" made national headlines. Publix suspended shipments from the dairy. Activists protested, and consumers made angry calls. Police arrested one of the workers, and the other three attempted to flee the country. These kinds of stories about the industry-at-large affected the public's views of Doyle's work. The ranchers' community relationships, though, had improved over the years.

In the past, environmentalists and ranchers stood on opposite sides of issues. "There was a fence between us bigger than the one Donald Trump is wanting to build," he said. "Over time, we've come more together. We're not 100 percent on the same page, but we do see we have a lot of the same concerns and are having enough dialogue to accomplish these things." He showed me an example of their common ground in a pasture dotted by skinny trees. About fifteen years earlier, Hurricane Charley hit the area and turned tall pines into stubs. They looked almost out of place in the vast, open field. The remaining pasture contained saw palmetto. Cows didn't like to eat the native plant, but companies used the palm's berries to create cancer treatment drugs. As one of the genteel cowboys told me, the berries were also used in "male enhancement drugs." Doyle could make more money if he cleared out the palmettos for improved pastures. He didn't do this because he thought it'd be bad for the land. "I'm speaking for most—but not all—ranchers," he said. "We consider everything involved with the land and the treatment of the cattle."

The ranches I visited were essentially small-scale, independently owned agricultural operations. I don't want to gloss over issues in industrial agriculture and factory farming, where huge corporations have been known to overcrowd animals. They can also exploit workers, especially immigrants. (Shortly after I visited these Florida ranches, Immigration and Customs Enforcement [ICE] arrested

680 undocumented workers at food-processing plants across Mississippi.) Real problems exist with industrialized food. These problems contributed to the appeal of FCR's homegrown beef. I wanted to write about Florida ranchers because of their important role in Florida agriculture. There weren't many other industries who shared such a close tie to Florida's history. The ranches I visited had centuries-long ties to the state.

Doyle and I left his pastures, and he asked if I liked to eat country cooking. "I'm talking really country," he said. I'll eat almost anything, so we made our way to his favorite spot, a little restaurant known for its fish fry and okra. The cowmen I met all enjoyed conversation over good food. The waitress knew Doyle and what he wanted to eat. I ordered the fried-everything.

I could tell Doyle had been at first skeptical of me—a journalist with a poet's soul. Throughout the day, he had carefully chosen his words. By the time we'd sat to eat, he seemed relaxed. He talked about the passing of his parents. He told me about the upcoming rodeo he planned to attend. His team hadn't performed so great in the previous one. He brought the conversation back to the cattle and his land. "People think we're tough, stoic guys—well, bull," he said. "I just want people to know we care about what we're doing."

I never thought I'd see a cowboy get emotional, but I understood why he did. He'd worked hard on the land and had seen how long it stretched. But he could only be responsible for where he stood, his plot. There was so much else out of his hands. So much he couldn't control. He would wake the next day with the sun and would do the same the next day until he couldn't anymore. He would try to leave the land better than when he found it. He'd do his best, and he hoped the next generations would have the chance to do the same.

*Y*OUNG AND
BEAUTIFUL FOREVER

The first boy I ever crushed on had the best tan in school and could perform a spot-on impersonation of Jim Carrey. I had to pine for my *Ace Ventura: Pet Detective* from afar because my Southern Baptist school considered homosexuality a sin. It was an expulsion-worthy offense. The high-school me feared expulsion for homo-feelings, but, luckily, I had Tampa. A bridge separated the city from God and the school's administration. My best friend Jessica and I would drive to the city's gay bars more often than I care to admit. We'd get drunk on our own kind of holy water as I began to figure out how this whole gay thing worked. I could do this as a young teenager in bars because I had found an ID of a twenty-five-year-old white guy with a crew cut. I'm not saying all white guys look the same, but the ID worked for me all but one of the many, many times I flashed it.

I struggled with my outlawed sexuality during the day, but in gay bars, I danced away the fiery damnation. In those bars, I got a different education. I heard a new language, code, and slang. I started to learn the history of men who had met in secret bookstores and clandestine spaces. Those generations had fought for people like me. I learned these things from older guys. They'd usually arrive at the club early like me—them to get home at a decent hour, and me to get in for free. I'd sit at the bar next to them, and they'd tell me a story. I've always liked good storytellers, and those seasoned queens were some of the best.

It was at one of these bars that I first dressed in full drag, for Halloween when I was seventeen or eighteen. I took inspiration from rock groupies. I put on a Joan Jett wig, AC/DC bandana, black lipstick, and drew skulls on my arm. I wore a tank top as a mini dress and let a lavender bra hang out of it because I'm classy. Halloween proved my one big foray into drag until I moved back in with my grandmother.

My hometown haircut place only took appointments for women, even though they also cut men's hair. My favorite stylist, Randy, called it an old barbershop rule. He gave me a code name to use for appointments. "Call in and say you're booking a haircut for Brigitte," he said, "that way I'll know it's you when I see the schedule."

The seasoned queen Randy cut my hair for years. We struck up a friendship through discussions of *American Horror Story* and the less popular Ryan Murphy show *Scream Queens*. "Mom said I'd been so traumatized as a kid that I'd grow up to be either a compassionate person or a serial killer," said the fifty-two-year-old. "Instead of turning into a serial killer, I just like to watch them on TV."

Randy Phoenix—his real, legal last name—is a seventh-generation Floridian. His grandparents owned a dairy farm that got turned into a cemetery in St. Petersburg. He never knew anything other than Florida, and his mom, like mine had, took him to the beach because it was free. His mother also took him to St. Petersburg's Webb's City, nicknamed "The World's Most Unusual Drugstore." He loved going to this mall before malls because he could walk through its mermaid grotto. The mermaids were made of plaster, but to him, they were beautiful. "I've known since I was a tiny, little kid," he said, "that I liked mermaids and shiny sequins."

At five years old, he moved with his family from St. Petersburg to nearby Pinellas Park. The areas, while adjacent, were worlds away in terms of diversity at the time. Pinellas Park residents were more country to him. Everyone seemed to own a truck with a Confederate flag in the back of it. People bullied Randy for being effeminate. A boy gave him a black eye during a middle school book fair, then continued to assault him until senior year. Randy faced daily harassment in the school; even his teachers teased him. His math teacher made fun of his bright socks in front of the whole class. A few of the teachers at my Southern Baptist high school had teased me, too. An English teacher nicknamed me "Skittles"—as in "taste the rainbow"—and a math teacher told me I sounded gay. Randy experienced violence that I never did. He ran for his life almost every day.

His bus driver often let him off early so he could start running before the other kids had a chance to chase him down. If they had social media back then, the online bullying may have pushed him over the edge. "I don't think I would have survived it," he said. "I'm not sure I'd be here right now because it was that bad for me at times."

In senior year, he stood up to the boy who had assaulted him since the middle school book fair. One day the boy came up to him in the locker room and said, *hey faggot, come suck my dick*. Randy responded with, *I'm going to beat your ass in the bus circle so everybody can see a fag beat you up*. The two met outside and Randy went into a rage. He "blacked out" and broke the bully's jaw. The boy's family took Randy to court. He said the judge told them they needed to teach their kid some manners. He dismissed the case. The school suspended Randy. After the fight, he didn't feel safe enough to return. His mother went into action mode. She had supported him since they'd walked together through the mermaid grotto and, later, when he walked in her heels. She wouldn't allow this experience to define her son. She told him, *you're not going back to that school, anyway. I've got you enrolled in something better—a beauty school*.

This beauty school intervention forever changed Randy's life. It also changed his makeup routine. He met his first drag queen through beauty school friends. He had never met a queen, but he fell in love with the illusion. Necessity may be the mother of invention, but, for Randy, the mother of invention was drag—his ticket into gay bars. He'd been sneaking into Tampa gay bars until a club's staff member discovered he was underage. The next time he went there, a "raspy-voiced lesbian bouncer named Fruity" wouldn't let him in the bar. He didn't know what to do, but his friend had a fabulous idea. He told Randy to get up in drag and go back over there.

Randy threw on a bleach-blonde wig, some makeup, and a Cindy Lauper–inspired outfit. He adjusted his skirt and approached Fruity, the guardian of all things gay. She met him with the universal gay greeting of, *hey, girl*, and let him into the promised land. The staff didn't recognize Randy, and he began to perform in the bar as his eventual drag persona Porscha. Porscha soon made as much money doing drag as Randy did doing hair.

Randy, who preferred male pronouns when not in drag, worked as Porscha all over Florida and participated in drag pageants. She was known as the "funny, fat girl," and emceed shows. Porscha found out she loved the spotlight and being on a microphone. Randy described those nights as a mess, but he found a community among all the lipstick and lashes. He also found himself. "When I was in drag, I was empowered," he said. "I never felt uncomfortable like I couldn't go to a Circle K in drag because I was going to make them like it no matter what."

Drag soon became a family affair. Both his mom and dad attended Porscha's shows. They even let his friends get ready in their home. They'd all sit around the family table to put on their faces. The friends would cut up and carry on for hours while Randy's dad sat back in his recliner laughing along with them. These family nights of the eighties halted during the latter part of the decade. "AIDS did not miss the Florida area at all," said Randy. "I don't think people grasped the magnitude of what was going on because they didn't see what they were seeing in the big cities." His three best friends died from the disease. He went to a succession of at least seven funerals.

As a late-eighties baby, I grew up in the wake of the AIDS outbreak. I feared I could catch the disease from a finger prick at a gas pump. I also thought I could become gay from sitting in the same place as a gay man. In my adult years, I began to write about men affected by the AIDS crisis. I couldn't imagine the trauma they experienced, the sheer number of people who died around them. I interviewed queer men who lost partners to the disease. One man told me he stopped keeping the death toll of his friends after thirty of them died from AIDS. "It was a freaky time," said Randy. "You just never stop thinking about it. It never goes away." The AIDS crisis changed nightlife and the LGBTQ community forever.

Randy continued to perform in drag throughout this scary time. He most likely would still be performing if he hadn't hurt himself. He fell into a drained swimming pool and damaged his back. He could no longer stand in heels, so he hung them up for good. He has since felt like a big part of him went missing. He thrived on the applause and had found a family with the performers. "Now that I am growing old in Florida," he said. "I don't know who is going to care that I'm gone. The older gay people I know have no one to look after them or to help take care of them. They have to make plans for themselves, which I'm not very good at for myself."

Randy's injury led him and his partner of twenty-one years to my hometown. He called the area one of the most conservative places in the county. "But believe it or not," he said, "a lot of gay people come in the shop." The area was miles better than the days when he ran for his life after school. "There's still a ton of stupidity, but it's more open than when we were kids," he said. "No matter where you go, you're going to see a gay person. People have really started to come around to it."

One person who helped Floridians come around to the LGBTQ community was Nadine Smith. She cofounded Equality Florida, the Sunshine State's largest statewide LGBTQ civil rights organization. She was also a founding board member of the International Gay and Lesbian Youth Organization and served on the U.S. Commission on Civil Rights Florida Advisory Committee as well as received awards from agencies like the League of Women Voters.

I had first heard Nadine's name about a decade before I met her. I was an undergraduate at the University of Central Florida, and I had joined what was then called the Gay Lesbian Bisexual Student Union (GLBSU). The GLBSU hosted meetings, participated in activist demonstrations—like same-sex mock weddings—and planned fundraisers. Some of the club's more activist-y members interned or volunteered for Equality Florida. I set off on a different path and interned at the local LGBTQ newspaper. I heard Nadine's name discussed as an activist icon in Florida.

I met up with Nadine in Randy's hometown of St. Petersburg. Parts of the city had become cool and hip in the previous decade or so. We walked through an area of downtown once called a ghost town. Upscale salons, dessert bars, and restaurants now lined its streets. Nadine's a heavy hitter in activist circles, but she's also down-to-earth and, like, really cool. A passerby stopped to greet Nadine. Then another person did the same. And another. More than twenty-five years of activism helped her become a recognizable face of both warmth and fierceness.

Nadine was born up North in Maine, one of only thirteen states the Air Force would station her father in the sixties. He had a supposed integrated marriage. "My wife was black, too," said her father, George, "but they were ignorant. We'd been married in England, and they didn't know black folks were in England." The family jumped around overseas and across the United States for a decade.

They settled in Callaway, a small town in the Panama City area of north Florida. They had always lived in more liberal areas. George said the racism he experienced in north Florida proved a cultural shock. "I had heard about riding in the back of the bus," he said, "but it was the first time I ever saw a colored drinking fountain." George struggled to find a place for his family to live. Early sellers rescinded contracts because of his race. He bought a place in a neighborhood "black folks had never lived in before."

Nadine finished high school in Panama City as a top student, but she didn't plan for a life in activism. She saw two paths: one, a career in the Air Force like her father, and the other as a muckraking journalist. She decided to follow in her father's footsteps. She enrolled in the Air Force Academy in the eighties, pre the "Don't Ask, Don't Tell" policy. The academy, she said with an ironic laugh, was a "terrific place for a young lesbian to struggle with her sexuality." People got kicked out of the military for their sexual orientation. They faced dishonorable discharges and crushing financial burden.

Nadine left the Air Force Academy and decided to eat nails with us journalists. She began to cover city politics. For an early assignment, she covered the failure of a human rights ordinance. She heard Council Members use homophobic slurs and wanted to help the cause. She quit the paper and wrote press releases for organizers. One day, someone didn't show up, and she gave the speech with the "page shaking, half an inch" from her nose. A newspaper article described her as "activist Nadine Smith." "I thought oh, there's no certification process," she said. "You just show up, and I've just been showing up ever since and encouraging other people to do the same."

At the time, activism focused more on the national level than on local issues. The Human Rights Task Force of Florida began to change the state conversation in the early nineties, but no true statewide LGBTQ group existed in Florida. Then, Nadine met Stratton Pollitzer, who described her as "one of the visionaries in this movement." Stratton remembered the early days when "the far-right would bus in hundreds of people" to protest pro-LGBTQ policy. These protesters outnumbered him and Nadine. They founded the nonprofit Equality Florida in 1997.

Florida played an important role in southern politics. A lot of people didn't consider Florida part of the South, but the state's laws and leadership often aligned with neighboring Bible Belt states. Republicans held a supermajority for almost twenty years. They controlled cabinet positions, the Governor's Mansion, the House, and the Senate. "From a political standpoint, Florida is a southern state," said Stratton. "You just need to look at our state government and the partisan balance in Tallahassee." Parts of Florida might take issue with being called the South. Stratton said the state "needs to acknowledge we are a southern state because when we win here, we want it to be the breakthrough for the South."

Equality Florida grew from a two-person operation to one with about thirty staff members. They covered areas from north Florida and the Panhandle to Key West. "We have been able to kill or neutralize every piece of the many homophobic bills filed," said Stratton. The organization helped pass human rights ordinances, same-sex marriage, and adoption legislation. It also developed transgender inclusion initiatives. Nadine was central to these efforts, and she faced pushback at almost every step. "If she was a white guy, I don't know if that would happen as much," said Elizabeth Schwartz, co-counsel on several key lawsuits that helped end Florida's adoption ban. "People like Nadine articulate the work that still needs to be done." This work took a life-altering shift on June 12, 2016, when a gunman killed forty-nine people and wounded fifty-three more on Latin Night at Pulse, an LGBTQ nightclub in Orlando.

When people find out I'm gay and lived in Orlando, they sometimes ask me if I knew anyone who died in the Pulse shooting. This question always shocks my system, and I try to change the subject.

I don't tell them that after Pulse I awoke to a panicked voicemail that my friend Christopher "Drew" Leinonen was missing. Drew and I had been close friends in college, and we'd known each other for about eight years. We'd bonded over a love of pop culture and a penchant for intense discussions about life. He was one of the first people I ever talked to about getting sober. We had most recently hung out when he visited New Orleans in my last year of grad school. He drove up from Florida with his boyfriend, Juan Guerrero, and their friend Brandon Wolf. Drew and I sat on a balcony in the French Quarter as the sun cast shadows down alleyways full of revelers. Everyone seemed so happy that day. And we were, too. We talked about who we had been in college and who we wanted to be in the future. "I know we don't talk as much as we used to," he said, "but I love you." I said I loved him as well. That was the kind of friends we were, and the kind of friends I thought we'd always be. That night, I met him at a gay club in the Quarter, and we danced to pop remixes. There was nothing better than high-kicking next to a good friend when the dance beat dropped.

I thought about that New Orleans night as I drove to Orlando soon after the Pulse news. I lived about 2.5 hours away from the city with my grandmother. I felt compelled to help my community in the best way I could, and that meant I had to report on what happened. News stations set up tents near the club, so I drove to a hospital. At that point, Drew was still missing. He'd been at Pulse with both Juan and Brandon. There were fewer reporters at the hospital, and the first person I heard speak was a victim's father. I talked to a man, sobbing; his two friends were still missing. As the hours went on, the death toll increased. One friend told me he knew someone who lost five friends that night.

A few days after the shooting, I got ready for Drew and Juan's joint funeral.

The gunman killed them both in one of the largest mass shootings in U.S. history. I don't remember a lot about those days, but I do remember someone told me members of the Westboro Baptist Church planned to protest my friends' funeral. The thought of them being there turned my stomach. I didn't see any protestors at their funeral, and I'm not sure if any were there. I had tunnel vision the whole time and a ringing in my ears. When people ask if I knew any Pulse victims, I don't tell them any of that. I don't tell them the great things Drew and Juan could've done if they'd only had longer to live.

Brandon Wolf had been at Pulse with Juan and his best friend, Drew. He'd separated from them to use the restroom when he heard a strange noise, something like a firecracker. Many patrons thought bangs were part of the music before they realized they were gunshots. Brandon and others around him decided to grab hands. They linked arms with whomever they could and ran to the emergency exit. Brandon was able to escape while Drew and Juan remained trapped inside. He later found out his friends had died, and grief overtook him. He'd never felt such heartbreak; it was the first adversity that challenged his resolve and faith in humanity. At Drew and Juan's funeral, Brandon struggled to figure out the words to say goodbye. He gripped his best friend's casket. Before he let go, he thought, *I'm never going to stop fighting for a world you'd be proud to live in.*

Those words have shaped Brandon's life since then, and one of the ways this promise manifested was in his helping cofound a nonprofit. Brandon and several of Drew's friends—some of whom I know—wanted to continue Drew's legacy, so they created The Dru Project (Drew often went by "Dru" online). The nonprofit focused on LGBTQ youth, specifically high-schoolers as Drew had founded his school's Gay Straight Alliance. The Dru Project has funded scholarships and grants as well as published one of the country's most comprehensive GSA guides. "The vision has always been keeping the best parts of Drew alive," said Brandon. "No matter who you were or how you loved, Drew made you feel like you belonged."

Brandon hadn't been much involved in politics prior to Pulse, but he, like Nadine Smith, began a life in activism by showing up. He called Nadine the "oracle" and remembers when she first reached out to him to discuss funds for survivors. In the aftermath of Pulse, an Equality Florida staff member set up a GoFundMe campaign, and nearly 120,000 people donated to the cause, which raised more than $7.8 million. These funds were designated for victims, some of whom were undocumented or in relationships not legally recognized. After their initial conversation, Nadine became a mentor to Brandon as he began to use his voice for advocacy. He spoke at the Democratic National Convention, contributed op-eds to national publications, and appeared in segments on MSNBC and CNN. He also traveled with Elizabeth Warren during her presidential campaign. Equality Florida eventually offered Brandon a full-time position, and he quit his thirteen-year-long career at Starbucks to dedicate his life to the cause. "We have a lot of work to do in Florida," he said. "The state is on the cusp of doing some incredible things, but we've still got to do the work."

Nadine and Equality Florida have approached this work—on issues like rational gun policies and LGBTQ civil rights—through bipartisan relationships. These cross-aisle conversations had become a staple of Nadine's life. She had spent her life dealing with people who didn't agree with her, like her father early on. They had a falling out because of her sexual orientation, but he eventually came around. Now, George Smith, a member of his church's choir, couldn't be prouder of his daughter. "We worked all that out," George said. "I support her 1,000 percent because I think she's right." If a church member asks him about Nadine's sexuality, he says, *she likes women just like I do.* The gregarious father even appeared in a marriage equality commercial alongside Nadine. As with George, a lot has changed in Florida, but there's still more work to do.

Nadine's job wasn't yet finished, and Equality Florida planned to usher the state into the future. The organization wanted to help with policy around hate crimes, bullying, and transgender rights. Nadine saw the future as filled with experienced activists and young, energetic people. Those folks looked to tomorrow, but they also expected a better Florida right now.

South Florida's Walter Latimer left Florida, in part, because he expected a better Florida right now. I reached out to him because the performer encapsulated a living Venn diagram of some of my interests: drag, sobriety, and Florida Man.

Born and raised in Miami, Walter grew up thinking he lived in the best city on earth. His opinion of the state changed in high school. "It started becoming clear that things in Florida were kind of backward," he said. He left the state and, like I had after college, migrated to Chicago, the Sunshine State's opposite. He enrolled at the School of the Art Institute of Chicago (SAIC). His studies became too expensive, and he dropped out of SAIC to enroll at my alma mater, the University of Central Florida. He stayed for a semester. "Orlando is the magical place" where he "got addicted to meth." Walter ping-ponged around Florida before he returned to Chicago, where he became, in his own words, a four-time art school dropout.

During this time, he was diagnosed as HIV-positive. The then twenty-one-year old began to watch *RuPaul's Drag Race* when he was "sick in bed with HIV." He had dealt with internalized homophobia as a child, and the TV show allowed him to experience drag in a different way. He filed drag on his back burner to focus on sobriety. He left Chicago to work in California. He felt lonely there and thought drag might help him make friends. "I was like maybe if I show up in a crazy look people will talk to me," he said, "and things just sort of took off from there."

Walter's drag queen persona Florida Man then arose from the ashes. He wanted to be referred to by his legal name when talking about his life and Florida Man when discussing drag performances. Florida had frustrated Walter as it had me so many years before as a pasty beach-walker. He, like most every millennial, had seen "Florida Man" headlines all over the internet. He decided to repurpose the meme. "Those headlines are the epitome of everything weird and strange about the state," he said, "but all the ways I describe Florida are ways I could totally describe myself." Walter's drag persona created a marriage of the things he cared about and valued like the absurdity and tragic comedy of Florida.

In an Instagram video, Walter as Florida Man sat in a bathtub streaked with blood. Red roses stood in a white vase and a sack labeled bath salts at the tub's foot. Florida Man stared into the camera and took a bite from a face. "Florida Man Eats Faces on Bath Salts" paid homage to an original viral Florida Man headline. Other Instagram videos showed her dressed in a Florida-shaped costume with "69" pinned to the Panhandle. In a mock weatherwoman clip, she repeated "scorcher." There were also photos of her as a vampire, deranged lion, and "Lady Voldemort"—the *Harry Potter*–inspired character who helped Florida Man achieve internet fame.

In 2018, Walter posted a performance of Florida Man dressed as the pale-faced and no-nosed Lady Voldemort. She danced a burlesque number to pop star Ariana Grande's hit "Dangerous Woman." The video made headlines, and the newfound attention propelled the drag performer to a surreal level. Venues flew her overseas to places like Glasgow and Dublin. She participated in a tour with famous drag queens from *RuPaul's Drag Race*, the gateway TV show for her drag. Walter received opportunities performers would kill for, but notoriety came at a crossroads. "I was on drugs the whole time," he said. "I was having a true 'Florida Man' moment because before the viral moment I was trying to move back home to get sober." He caved under the pressure and decided to go to rehab.

Walter's "Florida Man" experience changed his outlook on life, and it also changed his views on Florida. "People think everything is weird about Florida," he said. "Once I accepted it is a weird place, it was a freeing feeling." Walter, who is now in recovery, didn't know if he'd continue drag after rehab. He thought Florida Man may have already given him enough, but he ultimately decided he needed to utilize his newfound voice. He used his platform in a somewhat polarizing manner when he withdrew from a Pride event in 2019. A corporation funded the south Florida pride event. This corporate backing, he said, went against Pride's original grassroots efforts.

The LGBTQ community traced its Pride roots to 1969's Stonewall riots, described as a response to policing of the queer community. Activists organized the first Pride parades the following year to commemorate the event. I attended a few of these Pride parades over the years. The first ones I went to hosted floats from local bars and activist organizations. Dance music served as a soundtrack along with the revved engines of the "dykes on bikes" squad. Over the years, floats began to get sponsored by businesses and financial services. Lots and lots of financial services. For some, the mainstream attention resembled progress. Others voiced criticism of corporate involvement. They thought these Pride brands exploited the community. Walter didn't want to take part in this "privatization of Pride," so he withdrew from a performance.

Local Florida papers covered Walter's minor controversy. They cited an Instagram video he posted. Publications didn't reach out to him for comments, but they talked to people from the other side. Some in the community considered his decision bitter or misguided. Other people, mostly from cities outside Florida, reached out to express their support. "What I've noticed in south Florida," he said, "is people will throw their community under the bus for the sake of getting out of here." Walter had grown up with a similar way of thinking. He withdrew from the Pride event to "take a stance" for a community he hoped to help grow.

The owners of Vitambi Springs, a "Wilderness Resort & Camp" for men, had also made plans to help their community grow. "LGBT seniors have been forgotten," said co-owner Steve McCloud. He helped open the Florida campground with a goal to one day house LGBTQ retirees who faced unique issues in their swan-song years.

Florida was officially the Sunshine State and unofficially the retirement state. For a pale native like me, this meant I was an expert on two things: sunburns and senior citizens. My mom worked long hours as a waitress, so I spent many childhood nights with my great-grandmother, Granny Lula. She lived across from a shuffleboard court in her 55-plus mobile home park. I dreaded the beach because of sunburns, but I loved to play shuffleboard. I got good at pushing discs across a long, scratchy court into an opponent's triangle to score points. I'd venture out to the court on overcast days to see if I could strike up a game. The sweatband-wearing retirees weren't always too keen on a young up-and-comer crashing their afternoon. They still let me play with them. I, unironically, considered those players the coolest. They got to play shuffleboard all day, wear pastels, and eat dinner before 5:00 p.m.

A wave of LGBTQ senior citizens had begun to approach the shuffleboard life of retirement. Vitambi co-owner Martin Ruddock believed the community was not doing enough for the first generation who had lived their lives as out gay people. These folks needed different kinds of help than their straight counterparts. The seniors often didn't have children or a legal partner. Some of them didn't have long-standing social networks because of the AIDS crisis. "There are gay men who have no choice," said Steve. "They're not even honest with their doctor about their health concerns and go back in the closet to get quality health care." Steve said people didn't discuss aging enough in the LGBTQ community. They didn't talk about how to prepare for it. "We are young, beautiful gay men, and we think we will always be young and beautiful forever," he said, "but then it all fucking changes and nobody ever warned you."

LGBTQ retirement communities and housing efforts had sprouted up across the country, but Steve thought they could be more effective. He explained that a lot of programs designed as such housing "ended up being 30 percent LGBT at best." Programs with federal government funding were limited in LGBTQ accommodations. Guidelines didn't allow for discrimination in any direction. Developments couldn't be only for gay men as that would be discriminatory toward other genders and sexual identities. The use of federal funds also came with income restrictions, often below the poverty line. There was a large group of people in the middle financially but who weren't wealthy. "Those are the people I want to make the spot for," Steve said, "and I think it can be done if you've got the land, and that's what we've got here." The owners of Vitambi Springs wanted to expand their venture to a retirement community. They decided to start with a more manageable project—a gay campground in the unlikely destination of Clewiston, Florida.

My grandmother, whom I call Gramel, had wanted to make the trip to Vitambi Springs with me because some of our family members had lived in the same town as the campground. I didn't see a reason she couldn't join until I realized certain parts of the campground, like the pool, were clothing-optional. My grandmother and I are close but not that close. We agreed she should stay home.

On a Friday afternoon, I drove very much alone down a desolate road. I navigated a winding path of saw palmettos, cabbage palms, pine trees, and love bugs. The south Florida landscape resembled someplace a TV character like Dexter might dump a body. I finally arrived at Vitambi Springs. The property spanned 269 acres with thirty-three rentable units and fifty tent sites. It cost fifteen dollars to pitch a tent for the weekend. Furnished homes with three bedrooms, two bathrooms, queen-sized beds, and central A/C-heat ran for $250. I had, unsurprisingly, booked one of the air-conditioned rooms.

I parked in a patch of grass and walked into the main lodge, one of Vitambi's hubs. There was a small front shop with camping essentials like batteries, a dedicated bar, and a large dining hall at the lodge's back. Co-owner Martin Ruddock greeted me from behind the front desk. A piñata hung over his head for a later activity in line with the weekend's theme of "Caliente: Celebrating Latin Culture." Other weekend themes included "Jocks Summer Camp" and "Harness" for those into leather or other gear. There was also "Beartopia" (quick note for the straights: "bear" in gay slang refers to a burly, hairy dude, and, for context, I was closer to an "otter"—a thin, kind of hairy guy). Vitambi's name derived from a Swahili word very loosely translated as a group of proud people, and the decor throughout gave off a safari vibe with animal prints, pictures, and statues.

"It's a full house this weekend," said Martin. "It's going to be great."

Martin grew up on Boston's north side and graduated from Northeastern University. He worked for a mutual fund company after college, then transitioned into real estate. Martin came of gay age during the beginning of the AIDS crisis that decimated two generations of gay men. He remembered a time he'd go out at night, and if he didn't see one of his friends, he assumed they had gotten sick. A lot of the men he knew retreated, and it was rare for him to see men in Boston over the age of thirty-five. During that time, he vacationed in Fort Lauderdale and felt a connection to the area. He met older gay men in Florida. They were in their late fifties, sixties, seventies, or older. They were tan and rocked Speedos. Martin saw a future he hadn't thought existed. "The generation most impacted by AIDS," said Martin, "came to Florida, at least what was left of them." He said this influx of gay men in Florida came about when certain gay men cashed in their insurance policies. They thought their days were numbered, so they decided to go to Florida, someplace where it's beautiful year-round. Some of these men moved to the state "on their last legs," then realized, *oops, I spent my life insurance policy, so I guess I live here now.* "In hindsight," Martin said, "so much happened so quickly." Martin thought he'd move to south Florida someday, but the 9/11 tragedy in 2001 accelerated his plan. Two flights had left from his hometown of Boston. He decided he should no longer put his life on hold.

He moved to Fort Lauderdale and started a property management business. Martin didn't know anyone in Florida, and he found it difficult to create a community. Fort Lauderdale proved a transient place where people came and went. "Back then in Fort Lauderdale," he said, "it was either a trick [a hookup] or they were just here for vacation." Shortly after his move south, his mother passed away from cancer. Martin spiraled. "It was very tough, and I crawled into a hole," he said. "That's why it was so important when I met Steve."

Vitambi's co-owner, Steve McCloud, had grown up in Nashville, Tennessee. He was "kind of out" in high school. He played on the football team, and his gay friends told potential bullies *if you have a problem with me, then see Steve McCloud about it.* He worked in a gay bar during college at Vanderbilt and found tolerance, not oppression, in the area. Steve graduated from Vanderbilt and moved to New York, then later to San Francisco. He ran a conservation corps in California that took kids out into rural areas to build horse trails. He and his partner eventually traded California for Key West to get as far away as the land would let them run. "Every weekend 20,000 new people were in town who had no idea who I was," said Steve, "and they assumed I was a tourist as well, so it was a very different setting. Anonymity was refreshing."

Martin and Steve met online. This was typical because many gay men in Fort Lauderdale met online or in a bar. The two became fast friends, and they leaned on each other when Steve's partner of twenty-four years died. "When you go through something like that together," said Martin, "you're bonded for life." They grieved with each other. After a while, they decided to go into business together as well. "We were both in a situation where we had to turn a page," said Martin. They talked about creating a property management business, but neither felt passionate about it.

Steve wanted to open a gay campground for adults. He had run the conservation corps in California and loved seeing people awaken to the spirit of the outdoors. Gay campgrounds are an actual thing, and I had visited one near Orlando before my Vitambi Springs trip. The website GayCampingUSA listed nearly fifty stateside gay campgrounds. Other ones in Florida included Sawmill, Camp Mars, and Camp David. Red states, like Georgia and Texas, also had multiple campgrounds. Steve brought this campground idea to Martin, who loved it. Southwest Florida and its endless tourists seemed like a perfect fit. The two looked for property in Key West, but they couldn't find anything affordable. They stopped looking for an already-built campground, but destiny had other plans. Steve found a former juvenile rehabilitation camp in Clewiston, close-ish to both Fort Myers and Fort Lauderdale. He and Martin, with a third partner who had since parted ways, acquired the land. They spent a year renovating and securing permits.

The team opened the doors of Vitambi Springs in 2011. Vitambi functioned as a men's-only campground for forty-eight weeks out of the year. Two weeks were designated for the women-only "babes in the glades," and all were welcome during the holidays. A lot of people Steve knew in Fort Lauderdale thought Vitambi would find a hotbed of gay hatred in that part of Florida. But they hadn't seen a hint of it. "People have been OK with us," said Steve. "I only detected one time when people thought we were snotty or uppity gay men."

I asked Martin about their decision to designate certain areas as clothing-optional, or, as Gramel called it, "the nude place." I wanted to know their thought process as "clothing-optional" might look shady to some people. If I'm ever faced with such an option, I always choose "clothing." I grew up Southern Baptist, and I'm a slight germaphobe, which I should probably address with a therapist at some point.

"We talked to a lot of people about it being clothing-optional," said Martin. "I was surprised by the intensity of people's opinions on both ends of the spectrum." Some people told Martin they wouldn't go to the campground if it was clothing-optional. Other people wanted to be able to walk around the whole campground in a birthday suit. Martin developed an armchair theory about the divide. "It's a generational thing," he said. The over-fifty crowd pushed for clothing-optional everywhere, and the younger guys—the ones who weren't nudists—didn't want anything to do with it. "The real hard-core people tended to be older and had lived their lives in the closet," he said. "There's this sense of freedom they can get from being nude."

The clothes-wearing Martin and Steve manned the Vitambi ship with four other people. Steve took care of the facilities, the buildings, the landscape, and marketing. Martin handled the front of the house. They both worked on budgeting and finances. "If you would have told me when I was in Boston that I'd be on the edge of the Everglades in a men's resort," said Martin, "I would have said you were nuts. But here we are."

At dinner that night, Jay rang up my two tacos. He had a shaved head and wore a mesh T-shirt. He told me he'd driven to Vitambi from south Florida's Wilton Manors, a city with about eleven thousand residents. Wilton Manors was the first city in Florida to elect an all-LGBTQ city commission. Its website cited census data to claim it as the "second gayest city in America" (the gayest being Cape Cod's Provincetown, or, as most gay men call it, "Ptown"). Jay had volunteered to help with dinner. "You get addicted to coming here," he said. "Addicted and a dick. Boys will be boys."

I'd been out long enough to know that certain gay men often spoke with a running theme/joke/undertone of sex. This was probably due to our identity formation around sexual orientation and/or a general desire for sexy times. Body geometry propelled some of the guests, but Martin told me he'd known people who found long-lasting friendships at Vitambi. "It's difficult, still, to make friendships with people who are forty-five and older," he said. "It's hard to meet people outside of a bar, and yes, we have a bar here, but this is a whole different setting." The campground allowed for an escape from the urban chaos and a place to meet men under different circumstances. Vitambi's guests could talk outside by a campfire instead of in a thumping loud bar. There wasn't great cell service, which forced them to take a moment of reprieve from the anxiety of city living.

Jay introduced me to some of the city-living guys in the dining hall. A man from Toronto worked in higher education and gave me recommendations for scholarly journals about teaching. I sat with a real estate agent and a guy who went to school for design. I ate near a guy who worked on the business side of the porn industry. I chatted with a retired art teacher as well as a former 911 operator.

As guys headed to do whatever they planned to do, I talked to Manny and Francisco, a couple who had been together for forty-four years. The two met in a New York gay bar. Manny had worked in IT, and Francisco, a "playboy" at the time, worked in the mental health field. They grew to hate New York winters. They moved to Florida because of the state's weather and to live closer to South America.

The seventy-four-year-old Francisco immigrated to the United States from Ecuador at the age of fifteen. He became of legal age in the States and joined the army to serve in Vietnam. On his return, he used the GI Bill. He attended community college, a four-year university, then completed his master's degree and finished a doctoral degree. "I've dealt with many situations in terms of being gay, a minority, and a professional," said Francisco. "You get over all those things and look at the environment and say, 'really, I am going to show you who should be on the other side of the table.'"

Francisco's most challenging professional situation occurred on the morning of September 11, 2001. His day started off like any other until he got a call from his boss about something going on downtown. He sprinted to the terrace of a New York City hospital. He saw smoke. Francisco went into action mode and took charge. He's bilingual, and "a lot of people who worked in the towers were Latinos and their relatives didn't know English." From that moment until December he assisted New York City's mental health services. People in his hospital started to cancel their appointments. They were scared to leave their homes. On those long days, he'd do his best to compose himself, but then someone would show him a picture. They'd tell him, *this is my son, and he never came back.* He often cried in the bathroom.

As he approached retirement, Francisco wanted to leave the city.

He decided to move with Manny to Fort Lauderdale where there was a lot of support for the LGBTQ community. The couple discussed having children, but they decided against it. "We don't feel we are less privileged because we don't have a child to take care of us," said Manny. "We have friends who have seriously thought about having children to have someone to take care of them as they got older, but that's not for us." The couple knew they weren't going to have children, so they prepared for retirement early. "It's a process," said Francisco. "You have to get in touch with where you are financially and emotionally. You have to reevaluate yourself." Francisco spoke matter-of-factly. He looked me in the eyes, and said, "One thing I always tell my people is to have no regrets. If you reach my age at seventy-four and have nothing, still be happy. Don't feel victimized. The worst thing you can do is to become your own victim."

The couple and I talked about life and death, but we also talked about divas—like Cher and Madonna—friendship, family, and tactics to negotiate a raise as Francisco had done in New York City. This conversation reminded me of the ones I had during my formative gay years. The Florida gay bars I lived in back then always offered a mixed crowd. I learned the ins and outs of gay life from "the elders." Since those days, Francisco had seen a shift in gay culture. Phone applications and the loss of physical gay spaces, like those bars, created some division. Francisco said he experienced ageism in the community. "Young people shouldn't call me a dinosaur and look at people like oh, they're too old," he said. "They should use them as a tool to learn. They should pay attention to us."

Vitambi co-owner Steve McCloud said one reason LGBTQ seniors fell through the cracks was because people stopped paying attention to them. "I've been on this search for money to get involved in senior LGBT issues," he said, "and I'm surprised that the money is so hard to come by, and that there's not many gay men saying I want to adopt this cause." Expensive infrastructure proved one of the main challenges for such an expansion. Vitambi would need to bring in power lines, transformers, septic systems, and roadways. These kinds of projects need more than community interest. They need investors, and investors want returns. "I think it takes a celebrity like

Ellen DeGeneres," said Steve, "somebody to step up and say people just have no idea how horrible it is to die alone and die in a system that has no respect for you and your gayness."

Steve recounted a conversation he'd had with a friend whose partner passed away from complications due to Parkinson's disease. The friend had taken a caregiver's class, and everyone thought he attended it for his mother. "It was full of people who didn't understand he was going to be taking care of a man," said Steve. "There were no specifics for his situation." Steve imagined a few different models for sustainable LGBTQ senior housing. Some of them would cost a whole lot of money. He planned to speak to people who had a pension plan or inherited money. He hoped to place them in one-bedroom apartments and send a nurse by every week. "We've started to die away as a community," he said. "I talk to people all the time about this issue, and they say, 'gosh, I would love to be around like-minded people and feel that sense of security as I get older."

The Vitambi team could also build cabins designed for seniors. Steve called these "granny pods." They came equipped with special accommodations like thoughtful lightning, wheelchair-accessible sinks, and sensors to tell if someone fell. Steve also saw a type of independent living where a bunch of guys lived in the same space. Someone would cook every Thursday night, and someone else would do the laundry to make a few extra bucks for his magazine habit. Even this plan would be difficult. The concept of affordable housing in America has continued to change. People once relied on pension programs and social security, but, as Steve pointed out, such programs have started to disappear. People worked part-time or temporary jobs that paid by the hour and offered no benefits. It was getting harder to grow old with dignity, LGBTQ or otherwise. "That's just the way it will be," said Steve, "until this becomes a subject people are talking about."

The Vitambi team hoped to get people talking about aging. They wanted to help change the reality for their community, but they didn't know how successful they would or could be. People seemed to care about senior citizens only when they became one. The owners of Vitambi couldn't predict the future, but they knew we needed to look out for those who had helped us get to the present.

BRIEF ENCOUNTERS WITH ALLIGATORS

An airboat captain for Everglades Holiday Park reminded passengers that any animals we encountered on our trip were real. They were living in their natural habitats, and we shouldn't try to catch them on this February day. The captain then revved the boat's twin Cadillac engines. The combined 750 horsepower vibrated my bones as we sped into south Florida's Everglades. We soon reached a channel, and the captain slowed the airboat down to a meander. He pointed to monogamous swamp hens. He talked about other animals, but I got caught up in creating a romantic comedy for the idealistic birds. I started to get sleepy in the peaceful middle-of-nowhere Florida. I jolted awake when an alligator suddenly surfaced near the boat.

A tourist next to me positioned his iPhone close to Bubbette. The 5-foot-long gator used to be named Bubba until someone saw her being affectionate with a male gator. Bubbette seemed unbothered by the airboat. She hardly noticed as cameras clicked. I had once feared these reptiles. Growing up, I often saw them in a nearby lake I ran around for exercise. I'd spot their snouts in the water and pick up my pace.

Alligators had scared me then, but they didn't scare my great-aunt Annie. She stood about 6 feet tall and would feed leftovers to the gators in her backyard pond. We called her property the jungle because she could grow almost anything. The gators enjoyed Aunt Annie's food almost as much as her family members did. We braved a potential gator bite for a home-cooked meal. *Shuffle your feet*, she advised those who left her place at night. *It'll make the gators get out of your way.* This may not have been the soundest advice, but such Florida wisdom helped me make peace with gators as all Floridians must.

The prehistoric alligators chilled on the peninsula long before the written record reflected their characteristics. Ponce de León's crew stumbled onto the gators and called them El Legarto—the lizard. They weren't actual lizards in the scientific sense, but I'm no scientist. And I still like to refer to them as lizards.

The *Florida Agriculturist* wrote about early Floridian run-ins with alligators. The paper talked about a Florida adventurer who "found these monsters so numerous" he had trouble getting his boat through the waters. The paper also wrote about a "young lady" who chopped off a snake's head and killed an alligator on her way home. And then there was "Commodore Root," who was "interrupted by alligators whose ugly heads popped up at every turn of the creek. Two of these monsters hissed and blowed around his boat with deadly intent." Commodore Root raised his unerring rifle. He shot until the "gators lashed the water furiously and sank to the bottom."

The gator's reputation grew with Florida's own. People wanted to see the mythical land and creatures for themselves. An early promotional piece described the state's "huge alligators basking in the sunshine on the low banks and shores." The piece went on to describe an alligator floating lazily down the river. Florida allowed people to come face-to-face with these prehistoric reptiles. They could also kill them if it suited their mood. The ad joyfully said a man "placed a rifle ball" through one of the gator's eyes and through his brain. This death shot set "the gator afloat." These brutal portrayals of early life raised questions with *Agriculturist* readers.

A Californian wrote into the paper and wanted to know how many alligators were raised to the acre in Florida. This inquisitive person also wanted to know "if people die more than once of yellow fever." I didn't find the paper's answers to the question of the Florida zombie people, although I did come across the paper's recipe for gator fertilizer: a mixture of "muck, shells, alligators, and fish." People also commented on the gator's taste. They noted that if it wasn't "for the prejudice against the cussed ugliness of the animal, the tail of a young alligator would rank as a delicacy."

Potential alligator-eaters arrived in the state via railroads. A gator expert told me the big lizards climbed onto railroad tracks. Entrepreneurs put some of these gators in outhouses. They charged a few cents for northerners to see them. Automobiles helped outhouse gators evolve into roadside attractions. These included Floridaland (with porpoise shows and Western-style shootouts), Frog City, Ocean World, and Gatorland. I, unfortunately, missed out on the peak roadside era. But I still got to watch mermaids at Weeki Wachee Springs. The most popular roadsides embodied mythological Florida landscapes described by early explorers. Other animals—like snakes and dolphins—proved a popular draw, but nothing beat the Florida gator.

Well, almost nothing.

Overhunting caused the population to dwindle. In 1967, the American alligator was listed as endangered. Legal protections helped them stabilize in the late eighties. People couldn't shoot gators willy-nilly like they once could in the state. It's currently illegal to kill, own, or capture an alligator without proper license and permits. The gator population bounced back, and they're no longer considered endangered. In 2019, an estimated 1.3 million gators lived among Florida's 21 million or so people.

As a kid, I had feared the gators so prevalent in the Florida landscape, but as an adult, I became fascinated with them. I began to research them and write poems about their natures. They're cannibalistic reptiles. Mothers protect offspring from hungry dads. This proved a useful metaphor for a poet raised by a single mother. About a third of a gator's nest gets destroyed by predators. Out of an average clutch of thirty-eight, about twenty-four hatchlings will emerge. Only ten of those will live one year. Five of those yearlings will reach maturity. Maybe it was their survival odds and daddy issues that drew me to them; those traits may have also been what made them mean.

No one can argue alligators aren't badass animals, but they, like Florida itself, are complex. In the dry season, they use their mouths and claws to clear out roots. Their tails beat marsh to create a mud burrow. The gator hole fills with rain and freshwater. This water gets drunk by snakes, insects, turtles, and birds. Animals depend on gators to stay alive.

The sight of a gator never got old, not even for the Everglades Holiday Park owner Clint Bridges. On my airboat day, I sat in his office, and he told me of his scars like the one from a black bear named Cuddles. "The bear used to run through my house in diapers," he said, "and slap our Shih Tzu in the face." Clint had a linebacker's build with a football field smile.

His father, George, grew up in a small Georgia town where there was one red light, and it was always green. George lived on a tobacco and cotton farm with his ten siblings. He dropped out of school in sixth grade to help support his family. After he turned eighteen, George moved to south Florida and worked as a foreman on a construction site. He built a home from the job's spare materials. He mortgaged this house and built an airboat in his backyard.

He started to run Everglades Holiday Park as the mom-and-pop era began to fade in the 1960s. Disney had hit the scene. "We weren't successful in the beginning," said Clint Bridges, who owned the park after George. "There were times when the water was turned off, and I'd have to go out to the canal to flush the toilet." Clint began to work at his family's business around the age of six, when he stood on milk crates to man the register. The Bridges family originally leased 29 acres from the state. They acquired another 10-acre parcel. The business took people on more than 300,000 airboat rides a year. His father passed on gator knowledge to Bridges, who worked with them early on in his life. "If you put it in the current-day context," he said, "it's probably unacceptable. But it was kind of just what we did."

The second-generation alligator wrestler explained his method, which I took at his word because I had no plans to corroborate his method or even get close enough to a gator to touch it. I'm not a fan of touching any animal with whom I'm not on a first-name basis; this rule, too, applies to humans. Clint told me alligators' eyes were located on the outside of their skull. They see peripherally, kind of like horses. He said their sightline helped him grab the gator and then tap it on the nostrils. Gators can close their jaw structure with about 3,000 to 3,500 pounds of pressure per square inch. If they get something in their mouths, they'll go into a death roll, consecutive 360-degree spins. They'll spin until whatever part of the body they want ripped off got ripped off. "To make sure that doesn't happen," said Clint, "I'd tuck a thumb up under his jawbone and press straight back." The gator would then close its jaw, and Clint would put his hands over the gator's eyes. "Then you have to put tape or rope around the mouth to secure it," he said. "Oh boy, you better make sure it's secure."

The last gator his park received was from Paul Bedard, a volunteer trapper who wrestled gators at Everglades Holiday Park twice a week. "Paul will go out and capture a gator and then we'll put it in the pit with the others," said Clint. "He rescues it instead of it being euthanized or turned into boots or a wallet."

I later watched alligators named Bandit, Leo, and Godzilla surround Paul. He knelt in a sandpit with, by my count, sixteen of them. Paul's gators piled onto each other. They sunned themselves. He grabbed one of the less sleepy ones by the tail and got the gator to open its mouth. "Alligator wrestling itself is not like wrestling on television," he told the crowd. "Some people really think there's going to be headlocks and body slams. I'm not going to kick, punch, or hurt the alligator in any way."

A group of cadets from the Massachusetts Maritime Academy looked on as Paul kissed a gator. The cadets chose to spend one of their three port days at the park. They thought it would be wild to go out in the Everglades. Retiree Dean Cross vacationed from Arizona and put the Everglades at the top of his Florida to-do list. Both he and the cadets didn't want to leave the state without seeing one of its legendary gators in person.

Paul had grown up in New England. He moved to the Florida Keys as an adult to tag and release sharks. He turned his attention to American alligators in the Everglades, the only place on earth they and crocodiles coexist in the wild. The American gators look like crocodiles with rounder snouts. They can grow more than 14 feet long and weigh more than 1,000 pounds. The reptiles ranged from Texas to North Carolina, but there's nothing more Florida than an alligator (although the "Florida Man Arrested for Allegedly Throwing Live Alligator into Wendy's Drive-Thru Window" probably ranks high up on such a list, too). Paul got his start a gator trapper. He swam in ponds, roped them, and dragged them on land. He videotaped his exploits and landed a TV show, Animal Planet's *Gator Boys*.

The docu-series followed him as he responded to calls from people with gator problems.

The gators in his live show reacted to him differently than the wild ones he caught on television. He said his alligators knew "the worst possible outcome" would be for him to "sit on its back for ten minutes telling bad jokes." His jokes were, admittedly, bad, but his gators didn't fight him over the punch lines. They ignored him. Gators are cold-blooded, and they can only exert a certain amount of energy before their body begins to fill with lactic acid. After that, they don't want to move much. "The gators in this pit won't try to defend themselves," said Paul. "They've been here long enough to realize I'm not going to hurt them."

Most of the reptilian performers in his show were formerly nuisance gators. Nuisance gators were the fluffy gators who found their way into Floridian's pools or homes. Alligator removal was free in the state; it didn't matter if it was 3 or 13 feet. "The state saves money and liability," said Paul. "They don't hire trappers, so there's no workman's compensation if your arm gets ripped off." The page "How to Be a Nuisance Alligator Trapper" on the Florida Fish and Wildlife Conservation Commission (FWC) website states that trappers are "primarily compensated by their marketing and sale of alligator products" and may also receive "a small expense reimbursement" from the FWC for each gator taken. Trappers could make a couple of thousand dollars off one grown alligator if they took it to a processing plant. The gator would get killed and skinned. They could keep or sell the meat as well as turn the hides into fancy purses, watch bands, and belts. Farms in Louisiana harvested alligators for luxury brands, and it took years for gators to reach size. Internet tutorials allowed licensed trappers to skip the middlemen. The graphic YouTube video "How to Skin, De-bone and Flesh Out an Alligator" amassed over 15 million views, while "Butcher a Massive Alligator" racked up 9.2 million views, and "Clean, Fillet, Debone and Skin an Alligator" clocked in at 23 million views.

Almost every part of the alligator could get sold, even the head, dipped in formaldehyde. I'd grown up seeing souvenir heads in gift shops and gas stations throughout Florida. These spots also sold gator feet attached to keychains and dead baby sharks in glass jars. I didn't think much of it back then, but as an adult, it weirded me out. An 8-inch head went for about $9.50 and an 18-inch head for about

$140. At a former job, someone had placed a small gator head in the office break room next to a cactus on a windowsill. Marbles replaced its eyes. I ate next to the head for months until one day I thought, *that's a decapitated head on a windowsill.* I did some research and learned small souvenirs could be made from gator teeth, but there was no way to get those teeth until the head had completely rotted. This information led me to promptly find a new lunchtime spot.

Paul, a skilled trapper, could make a lot of money from the sale of alligators, but he wouldn't sell or kill them. There weren't many nonkill trappers in the state. "Not many people are dumb enough to work thirty to sixty hours a week for free," he said. "Especially for an animal that wants to rip your face off the first time you meet it." Paul brought the nuisance gators to Everglades Holiday Park to give them a stay of execution. "The only money we take in is solely from a tip basket," he said, "and I spend it on their food and vet bills."

Across town in Hollywood, Florida, a group gathered to watch an alligator wrestler at the Seminole Tribal Fair. Billy Walker crouched down. He'd been wrestling gators for thirty years as part of the tribe's tradition.

Native Americans lived in Florida with alligators before the Spanish arrived. They were made up of many different tribes—like the Calusa and Miccosukee—and colonizers first called Indians the Seminoles. The United States attacked the Seminoles and related Indians during the first half of the nineteenth century. These battles have been referred to as the First, Second, and Third Seminole Wars, but the Seminole Tribe of Florida recognized them as one long battle. The war decimated tribes. American Indians were captured and removed to Oklahoma. Others were pushed deeper into the Everglades.

"We once had twelve clans," said Billy, "but now we're down to eight."

The remaining eight clans were Panther, Bear, Deer, Wind, Bigtown, Bird, Snake, and Otter. "There used to be an alligator clan," he said, "but after the war, there is no more alligator clan."

As a child, Billy hunted gators and "shot at them with a .22 Magnum." The bullet would ricochet off the water and knock them out. He would catch the gator with rope. "The gator would wear out and I'd carry him over my shoulders," he said. In the early 1900s, some of the surviving Seminoles settled into tourist camps. They sold crafts and wrestled alligators for income. "There was only like two or three tourists that would come to the reservation per week, but they would give me money to do a trick with it," said Billy. He continued the Seminole alligator wrestling tradition as a link to his ancestors.

He tapped his Tribal Fair alligator on the snout. The gator tossed back his head, like a dangerous hair flip. Billy chuckled. "You're a bad boy," he said. This gator, unlike Paul's, must not have been around Billy long enough to know he wasn't going to hurt it. It seemed pissed. "This is extremely dangerous," the announcer said, "so he is going to have to be very careful." Billy threw both arms to his side. He put his hand under the gator's jaws. He clamped its mouth shut. The gator, now even angrier, death-rolled. It broke free from Billy's grip. The gator hissed. It meant business.

"As you can see this gator uses his tail like a broom," the announcer said, "and his mouth like a dustpan. He's trying to sweep him." The announcer handed Billy a stick. He used it to touch the gator's head, then walked behind it. The gator whipped its tail, and Billy jumped over it. The announcer called this move "the Everglades jump rope." Billy maneuvered to sit on the gator's back.

Billy caught gators he wrestled in south Florida's Big Cypress area. He also trapped gators for other people. "Our cattle ranchers—the Seminoles have a lot of cowboys out in Big Cypress—ask us to remove them," he said. He would then take the gator to the house and keep it in a pit. He would feed it chicken and different things to get it ready for the show. "If it was off the reservation," he said, "they'd get shot and killed. We keep the gators alive for our shows."

He and his daughter often went out together to find alligators. They sometimes caught gators crossing the road. Billy would throw a rope over its mouth and sling it over his shoulders. He'd wear the gator out like he did as a kid.

In Mary Thorn's show, the Floridian had swum with forty-one alligators in a central Florida pit. She worked with the gators every day and knew which ones were the most aggressive. "I had a gator that on command would show his privates," she said. "Another, I could pick up and kiss right on the mouth."

Mary, in her mid-fifties, reminded me of my great-aunt Annie, who used to feed her backyard gators. I admired these Florida women because they didn't take bull from anyone or any animal. Mary cared for her first gator as a little kid. Her brothers owned a fish hatchery, and she fished gators out to play with her Barbie dolls. The mother of seven never wrestled gators, but she did wrestle people. In a past life, she performed professionally under the name Biker Babe as part of the Triple X Team. The Great Malenko, who made a name for himself in Championship Wrestling, had trained her. Mary carried on the Great Malenko's legacy after he died. She body-slammed people for almost forty years in the ring before she retired to perform with gators. "I have been bitten twice by gators," she said. "Once in the head and once in the knee."

As part of her show, Mary circled a gator to let it know they were about to perform. Things went fine until mating season. A female gator climbed into the enclosure, and Mary didn't know she was in there. The gator nabbed her by the head. Thankfully, there was a second person in the enclosure to save her. Mary's other gator bite occurred when she tried to show people how high gators can jump on land. An older woman tripped and fell into the pit. Mary stepped in front of the gator to help her. This gator bit Mary in the knee. "Most gator attacks won't kill you," she said, "but you will lose a part of your body, like if you're feeding the gator, you're going to lose your hand or your fingers or have some good scars on them."

Mary's job at the gator show led to the ownership of her first alligators. FWC staff members brought five little gators in an aquarium to her boss. He couldn't take care of them, so she decided to get her permit and take them home. The FWC said people could keep an American alligator for educational purposes, exhibition, or sale if they obtained the proper permits and license. "There's a lot of people who own gators without their neighbors knowing," said Mary. "They could be living next to you because in Florida you can get a license to keep a gator inside and do education with it." License applicants had to demonstrate one year and one thousand hours of substantial practical experience with the care of alligators or other crocodilian species. Mary's gators—Rambo, Oscar, and Alyssa—had been poached as hatchlings and kept in a dark closet for years. They had little room to move in the small aquarium. Mary said they'd been in the dark for so long their immune system was shot.

The gators couldn't function properly, so Mary began to give them physical therapy. She soon found out the extent of damage done by the darkness. They couldn't take the sun. "I had one sitting by the window," she said, "and the filtered light through the window actually killed the gator." (I asked Dr. Laura Brandt—senior wildlife biologist for the U.S. Fish and Wildlife Service—about the possibility of sun-sensitive gators. She said, "Perhaps, they would have some sun sensitivity initially like you would have if you were kept in the dark.") Mary realized the gators' sun sensitivity. She thought, *if humans can do sunscreen, then gators can, too.* That's how her gators ended up wearing clothes. She lathered them in sunscreen and dressed them in biker gear and a Santa outfit for Christmas. Somehow, she didn't lose a finger in the process.

Mary's permits allowed her to keep alligators until they reached 6 feet in length. She did not live on the required acres of land needed to keep bigger gators. Mary planned to rehabilitate the gators and then take them to a facility like Gatorland in Orlando. Mary did this for all but Rambo. She didn't want to drop him off at one of the professional facilities because of his sun sensitivity. She feared his weakened immune system would get him eaten by other gators. FWC told her she had to find Rambo a new home because of his size. As Rambo inched toward 6 feet, she found it difficult to part with him. Her son died during her battle for Rambo, and she became even more attached to the gator she had raised. "I decided I wasn't going to get rid of Rambo," she said. "They were going to have to shoot me before I got rid of him."

As Mary grieved the loss of her son, she applied and reapplied for permits. Her resiliency—along with the fact she lived with a big gator who wore clothes—caught the media's attention. She became known as "Florida Woman Fights to Keep Her Pet Alligator Who Wears Clothes and 'Rides' ATVs." When the first reporters arrived, Rambo got excited. Mary said he wanted to kiss them all. At first, Rambo's newfound notoriety hurt their cause. People said she put people's lives in danger. There wasn't anything illegal about dressing alligators in clothes. But people—like PETA activists—took issue with it, even if Rambo did look cute dressed in his Santa outfit. They called the clothes an act of animal cruelty. Mary didn't see the difference between putting a dog in a sweater and a gator in one. A lawyer soon took up her case pro bono, and he struck an agreement with the FWC. For her to keep Rambo, Mary couldn't have him perform in shows or at birthday parties. His mouth must get taped if she takes him out of her yard.

A few years have passed since Mary's victory to keep Rambo. She turned her five-bedroom house into a cross between an animal shelter and antique store. People hand her down knickknacks and sick animals. The number of animals she kept on her property changed almost daily. At the time we spoke, she had two litters of squirrels, three chickens, five dogs, and one potbellied pig that had roamed under her neighbor's house. And, of course, she kept her eighteen-year-old roommate Rambo.

Mary converted one of the house's rooms into Rambo's bachelor pad. He would most likely remain a bachelor forever. Mary said he called out for a girlfriend and everything, but he couldn't have one. "Because his immune system is shot," she said, "we don't know whether a girlfriend would eat him."

Cold-blooded animals aren't social in the same way as humans, but Rambo ate at Mary's dining table about three times a week. He opened the refrigerator whenever he wanted a snack. He liked frozen chicken and wouldn't eat it raw or stinky like other gators. Rambo slept in a bedroom like a kid except his bed was a pool. "If Rambo's sick, he'll want to sleep in my bed with the five dogs," she said. "I get maybe two inches of the bed, and the animals get the rest." Mary said she couldn't imagine life without Rambo, but she knew the lifestyle was not for everyone. Really, it's only for the slim percentage of people who truly understood a gator's nature. After Rambo's media attention, Mary noticed more people who wanted gators as pets or emotional support animals. "Gators don't make good pets," she said. "If you don't know how to take care of these animals, you do not need to have gators." Gators had their moods. The three- and four-foot ones might be nice for a while, but they "weren't always going to be so nice." "They bite," she said.

People might think it's cool to own an alligator, but they often weren't prepared for its reality. Mary thought Rambo would grow to about 19 feet. She'd begun plans to build a cement pool the size of his room. She became adamant about gators not making good pets. "Rambo suffers," she said, "because of what some humans did to him." "A lot of redneck guys come up to me," she continued, "and they go, 'I was out there last night, and we had this gator. We were doing this and that with it.' Well, that's harassing the gator, and you're doing something illegal. That's nothing to brag about."

Mary's dream job would be to own three acres of survival land out in the wild. She wanted to open a rescue for gators, the ones like Rambo who had been hurt by people. She hoped to someday open her own mini version of Orlando's Gatorland.

In a Gatorland gift shop, a tourist stopped and peered into a small tank of baby alligators. He pressed his hand to the glass and smiled. "Can I pay to feed one of these?" he asked the cashier. "I flew all the way from Wisconsin for my birthday to hold an alligator."

The birthday boy was not allowed to hold the gift shop's baby alligator. But Tim Williams, Gatorland's "Dean of Alligator Wrestling," asked me to hold a different one. Tim wore Coke-bottle glasses. His mustache and tan uniform made me think of a character from *Jumanji*. Tim took a gator from a tank. He held it so it couldn't twist its head around toward me like the girl from *The Exorcist*.

"He won't bite you," Tim said. "Go ahead and hold him."

"No, thanks," I said.

Tim didn't miss a beat. He put the baby out of sight.

"We'll have you sitting on a gator by the end of the day," he said.

I smiled with no intention of doing anything of the sort. I'm fundamentally opposed to holding any reptile of any kind at any time. Even at Gatorland.

Owen Godwin Sr. opened the park in 1949 as a roadside attraction. He'd grown up in Kissimmee on a place called Rattlesnake Hammock. He spent his childhood, fishing, hunting, and, like most anyone who lived on a place called Rattlesnake Hammock, chasing snakes. As Gatorland's origin story went, Owen bought 16 acres of land off Highway 17/92 and 441, the state's second-most-traveled highway at the time. He and his family cleared the land with tractors and mules. They dug up palmetto. He originally named the park the Florida Wildlife Institute but thought it sounded too much like a government agency, so he renamed it Snake Village and Alligator Farm. He eventually settled on Gatorland, and I think he made a smart choice because I'd never want to go to a Snake Village.

Back then, Orlando didn't have any theme parks. This changed in 1971 with the opening of Magic Kingdom. Orlando eventually became America's most-visited destination with a bunch of theme parks like SeaWorld, Islands of Adventure, and multiple Disney parks. There was also Bible-themed The Holy Land Experience and the gun-themed Machine Gun America, where visitors could apparently shoot an AK-47 and drive a tank. Endless hotels and fast-food franchises have been built on former swampland, and a record-setting 75 million tourists visited Orlando in 2018. (Unfortunately, nature bumped up against fantasy in 2016, when a wild alligator snatched a two-year-old boy from a shoreline of a Disney resort. "It was a tragedy," said Tim. "Disney does everything they can possibly think of to make it safe for their guests. I don't think there's anything that they could have done or should have done—it just happened." After the boy's death, Disney reportedly took all the gators out of their exhibits.)

Gatorland sat smack dab in Orlando's theme park congestion. Its teal gator-mouth entrance served as a throwback to the golden age of Florida roadsides. Tim said Gatorland survived all these years, in part, because of its proximity to Disney. "When you get to Florida most people want to see beaches, Disney, and an alligator," he said. "And the best place to see an alligator is right here." He led me onto the park's boardwalk. I'd never seen so many alligators in one place. The boardwalk looked like a scene ripped straight from an *Indiana Jones* flick. The park had around 1,800 gators on 110 acres. They acquired a good many of their gators by way of trappers. "It's not like we need a gator," said Tim, "but it saves its life."

The park may save gators' lives, but not everyone was a fan. PETA once described Gatorland as a "notoriously cruel alligator park" where "visitors watched as the animals were forced to 'wrestle' with workers." These visitors could also eat gator meat. I'd eaten gator before, but I didn't want the Gatorland gators to see me eat their brethren. This meat didn't come from the gators who lived on their property. They got it from farms or trappers. "I love gators," said Tim, "but I will eat them. I think cows are cute, but I still like a good steak."

Tim grew up in Jacksonville, Florida. He took childhood trips to Ross Allen's Reptile Institute in Silver Springs. Ross was a leading

Florida naturalist of the time. He caught gators with his bare hands. He became Tim's boyhood hero. Tim captured rattlesnakes and sold them to Ross, who extracted rattlesnake venom for the medical field. "I took a box of snakes to him one day," Tim told me, "and he said, 'hey, come work for me. I was like okey-doke, I'll do that." Tim went on to work in a venom lab at an alligator farm until destiny led him to wrestle gators. The guy who did the wrestling show at the time broke his back, and they asked Tim to take over the job. Tim was more afraid of performing in front of people than getting on the back of an alligator. The crowd scared him to death.

Ross handed the wrestlers scripts. He wanted Tim to talk about certain things, like how the gator's nose and eyes worked. Ross gave Tim the meat of his performance, but Tim had to add the spices. This didn't come naturally for him, but he liked working with the reptiles. He began to add his personality to the show, and he became more comfortable in front of a crowd. He took his gator wrestling skills to Gatorland in the nineties.

Tim had worked at the park for about twenty-five years by the time I visited. He seemed to know everyone. He stopped to say hello to other employees and some of the park's regular bird photographers. "Before we built the boardwalk, there were no birds," he said. "Now, it's full of birds and nests. It's the only place they have to go." The park became a haven for wood storks, an endangered species protected in Florida. These birds had some groupies. Tim told me, "Birders are quite the industry, like an $8 billion a year industry." I filed away this birder information. I figured bird drama could percolate for me to write about later. I wanted to ask Diane Brannon, one of the Gatorland birders, about any of the industry's potential drama. I was dying to learn of the love triangles and offshore banking scandals. Instead, we talked about Florida wildlife. "Right now, the white ibis is breeding," she said. "We'll move into snowy egret season. If you've never seen the snowies in breeding plumage, it's awesome. It's just phenomenal."

Diane was a Florida transplant who married a third-generation "Florida Cracker." She drove an hour to the park. "All around here, you have so much going on as far as roads and cars and development," she said. "Birds are looking for safe places like Gatorland where they won't be threatened." Diane talked about the ospreys that built nests on light poles above the mass of traffic. "Florida is becoming overdeveloped, and it's really sad," she said, "but I've noticed, to a certain extent, some animals have adapted."

Tim had the energy of a man half his age. He ushered me away from Diane before I got dirt on the untapped drama of the birder industry. He wanted me to meet one of the park's most attractive specimens. His voice lowered when we neared the animal. It turned to a baritone when we arrived. "Crocodile! Croc, Sultan," he shouted. "Sul. Come here, buddy. Now, that's a good-looking crocodile, isn't he?" I couldn't yet tell a good-looking crocodile from an ugly one, but I nodded yes anyway.

"He's a Nile crocodile," Tim said. "A couple of those have been found here in Florida, and they shouldn't be here." These crocodiles were non-native and competed with everybody else. Tim thought these crocodiles might one day make it up to Texas from the Everglades. I'd heard news stories refer to them as "man-eating." I didn't want to hang around Sultan, whose name, full disclosure, I only connected to Egypt and the Nile much later. The park had to buy the Nile crocodiles, but they were often given gators for free.

One of these: a 1,000-pound gator named Chester.

Chester was a nuisance gator who had eaten a dog in Hillsborough County. He had faced the death penalty, but Gatorland staved his execution. Chester lived in an enclosure near an albino gator from Louisiana. Tim introduced me to one of his trainers who unlocked the door and led me to a grassy section at the enclosure's back. Chester chilled in the water. People watched from behind a pane of glass. Kids stared at the modern dinosaur. I stared at it, too. A man with a tattoo sleeve videoed us. Chester's trainer held meat, and the big gator slowly crawled up near us.

Chester was kind of famous. A video of him had gone semi-viral. In it, a trainer performed a trick where he stuck his hand in the gator's mouth, and Chester bit him. Now, Tim wanted me to take a picture near this same gator. I pretended not to hear Tim's request. Again. And again. I liked gators when we each had our own space. I knew Tim wouldn't put me in any real danger because he seemed kind. I also hadn't signed a release and could sue if anything happened. I stopped ignoring Tim and reluctantly inched closer to the gator. I wanted to show my appreciation for Tim and the time he'd spent with me. My manners may one day get me killed.

The gator hissed and forced air through his nostrils. I stepped back. Employees acted as a barrier, but I still felt the power of the ancient gator. I thought, *maybe this is the day he'll snap. Maybe today is the day he breaks free.*

Thankfully, it wasn't. But I still didn't take a picture with him.

Chester ate the meat and didn't pay any attention to us after that. He'd gotten what he wanted, and, apparently, humans bored him.

We left Chester and hustled over to the last stop of our day: the alligator wrestling show. Tim helped create the show, but he didn't perform in it anymore. "I've gotten to the point where I can get down on one of them," he said, "but I can't get back up." The park employed two alligator wrestlers. I assumed these employees received an impeccable health-care package because they also ran the Jumparoo show, during which they fed gators who jumped out of the water to grab meat. The wrestlers trained for at least ninety days before they officially entered the wrestling pit in front of an audience. "We start them out with tape on the gator's mouth," said Tim, "from that, they move into catching gators without tape." There's a big difference between tape and no tape, Tim explained; it's like riding a bike without training wheels.

I watched two of these wrestlers perform in a rodeo-type pit surrounded by a moat of water. This alligator show looked like a bigger-budget version of the ones I'd already seen. Performance value inched toward Disney-quality. One of the audience members near me asked her friend if the alligators were animatronic. The area's theme parks seemed to make people question reality. Florida, in general, has a way of doing that.

The gators were definitely not animatronic. They were real. Very real. I found this out firsthand after the show. Tim had told me earlier he'd have me sitting on a gator by the end of the day, and the end of the day approached. He convinced me to wait in line to sit on the wrestled gator's back. Tim wanted me to pose with it, most likely a nuisance gator spared from harvest by Gatorland.

I didn't want to crawl on the back of this gator. It probably wished for sleep instead of getting the paparazzi treatment. As my turn neared, I unexpectedly felt the urge to experience a fleeting moment as an alligator wrestler. Those Floridians understood these animals in ways I never would. I also felt peer-pressured by a circle of kids who casually took their photos with the animal. Their carefree giggles mocked me. I couldn't let them win, so I knelt in the sand.

The gator's mouth had been taped. I placed my hand under its jaw. I felt the softness. The head, in comparison, was rough. A shot of adrenaline rushed through my body. A lot in Orlando ran on an electrical impulse, but this gator ran on something different: a heartbeat. The gator's heart wasn't three-chambered like other reptiles. The big lizard had a four-chambered heart like mammals or birds—a long-lost dinosaur cousin. I rubbed my hand across the gator's head and felt grateful for it. These ancient gators contained Florida's history and the story of its land. They linked us to Florida's wildness—a wildness we should never forget.

$\mathcal{S}$NAKE SHADOWS

I followed snake hunters Leo Sanchez and Tim Meyer past a canal full of water lilies. Sawgrass stretched for years, and gnats pestered us like siblings. The bugs annoyed me, but they didn't worry me. My worry that January day was completely occupied by Burmese pythons. A chill in the morning air meant we might catch a python sunning itself in the Everglades.

At the time, the U.S. Fish and Wildlife Service had spent more than $6 million over seven years to address the growing problem of the invasive pythons in Florida. In 2013, the Florida Fish and Wildlife Commission (FWC) took a somewhat unconventional approach. They decided to let Floridians be Floridians. The FWC hosted the inaugural Great Python Challenge and let people hunt the pythons for cash rewards. Because of my lack of sense—as my grandmother would say—I signed up for 2016's second Challenge.

I contacted python hunters Leo and Tim through Facebook. They agreed to take me out to hunt snakes that can grow over 20 feet in length and weigh upward of 200 pounds. The two led snake-hunt expeditions for about three hundred dollars. One of their most interesting groups consisted of three women, a man, and a Japanese film crew. They'd gone out to hunt snakes for a game show. "The host wanted to be near a snake, but she freaked out," said Leo. "She knocked over the cameraman."

My best friend from high school, Jessica, agreed to come with me on the hunt. She was a real ride-or-die friend, both in the figurative and literal sense. Before we drove south, she applied for a gun permit. We thought one of us might need to shoot a huge snake to survive, and I surely wouldn't be the one to do it.

I had obsessively read about the invasive Burmese pythons. They had gone from south Florida tourists to permanent residents. A *New York Times* headline called them "The Snake That's Eating Florida." No one knew the exact number of wild Burmese pythons in the Everglades. They were secretive and difficult to find. Researchers estimated anywhere from thousands to millions of them lived in the Everglades. The Asian snakes thrived in the area. They ate birds and mammals and faced no real predators. The snakes had altered the ecosystem. In certain parts of the Everglades, raccoons and possums had decreased by 99 percent. The pythons even sometimes went after alligators. They, like other transplanted Floridians, competed for food and space.

I had first visited the Everglades as a child with my grandfather. The landscape reminded me of *Jurassic Park* with bugs as big as birds. I bathed in bug repellant. Nothing could ward off the near-fist-sized mosquitoes that postcards called our state bird. Despite those insects, I felt a deep fondness for the area. This part of my home state was a wonder of the world. I'd never been able to wrap my head around the sheer size of the Everglades. This area had once covered nearly 4,000 square miles with freshwater marshes, sloughs, and hardwood tree islands. In 1841, an anonymous explorer described south Florida as "one boundless expanse of saw-grass and water." It was occasionally "interspersed with little islands, all of which are overflowed."

The land resembled a vast sea. Those early explorers saw a dense forest, thick undergrowth, and sawgrass of "an impenetrable barrier." They trekked through mango orchards and avocado pear trees. They drank coffee at sunrise. They ate "wild turkey, broiled and fried curlew, plover, and teal, stewed crane, grecian ladies and fried fish." After they ate these spoils—some of which I'd never heard of—they used axes and knives to cut paths through scrub. The area abounded with "wild beasts, reptiles, and strange birds." They saw alligators so thick they "could walk across their heads." They swatted at mosquitoes, red bugs, alligator fleas, wampee, and "a thousand other horrors." One man wrote he saw a mother eagle "large as a goose" attack someone in his party five times, and on the sixth attempt the bird had a long hunting knife "driven in her neck." Explorers often exaggerated, but the nature they encountered probably appeared mythical. I know it did to me as a kid when I first visited the Everglades.

On my python trip, I pictured the Everglades as a late-1800s explorer described the area. "The snakes in front of us crawling out of our way would make such a crackling in the dry leaves that we would not be able to hear each other speak." Members of a similar expedition wrote they stepped around snakes. They were sometimes "struck by rattlesnakes of immense size, but their fangs could not penetrate the rubber suits." The explorers "soon got used to that kind of snake bite." They "thought nothing of seeing all manner of reptiles resting on some tree branch or a brush heap and ground."

I assumed Jessica and I would see the Burmese pythons hanging out everywhere. We'd come across gangs of them around every corner. They'd be waiting outside gas stations trying to get someone to buy them beer. Our drive to the Everglades had nearly confirmed my concerns. I spotted snakes on the side of the road and in bushes. I caught glimpses of them in ditches, ponds, and on tree branches. Snakes scared me, but I forced myself to look at each of them. I needed to know my enemy. I discovered those roadside snakes weren't actual snakes at all. They were more like snake shadows: old tires, plastic bags, and car parts.

The hunters we followed hoped to break the record for the longest Burmese python ever caught in Florida. At the time, this was slightly over 18 feet. Hunters weren't allowed to set up shop just anywhere. They could hunt in south Florida areas like Picayune Strand State Forest. Only authorized agents could remove pythons from Everglades National Park. The protected region encompassed 1.5 million acres. It was part of the largest subtropical wilderness in the United States. Competitors could only hunt during daytime hours. They submitted captured snakes either dead or alive to the FWC. Leo and Tim never killed snakes they caught. "It's not their fault they're here," said Leo. "They didn't gang up in Asia and say, 'hey, let's all go to the Everglades and fuck it up.'"

We walked by a canal, and Leo stopped. He jutted into the brush with a 40-inch snake hook, even though he didn't plan to use it. He preferred to grab pythons with his bare hands. "Usually, I find snakes so friggin' big," he said, "that I have to use an extra big bag to put them in."

☀

The thought of any size snake terrified me as much as I'm sure it did Jennifer Lopez in 1997's *Anaconda*, a film which I, of course, never saw because it's about a giant snake. As a Southern Baptist, I learned early on from Bible stories to never trust a reptile; a serpent tempted Eve in the Garden of Eden and look how that turned out. I've known people who love snakes, but my fear of them wasn't as irrational as some of those people had tried to make me believe. The reptiles were culturally associated with death, disease, or poison. Polls showed that anywhere from about 25 to almost 60 percent of adults in the United States faced some level of snake fear. Psychological scientists described this fear of snakes as "core mammalian heritage." The earliest mammals survived by learning to avoid reptiles like the *Tyrannosaurus rex*.

Our birthright as mammals was to fear snakes, but some people suggested a form of desensitization therapy to get over the phobia. One might begin this process by viewing many pictures of snakes to build up the nerve to eventually hold one. If one could hold a snake, the theory went, then one could understand the snake wasn't so bad. I understood this line of reasoning, but nothing like that would ever work for me. I literally couldn't look at pictures of snakes online without wanting to run out of the room.

The great thing about snakes, though, was that they could be avoided. People could move someplace like Antarctica where it's too cold for them to survive. But the warm weather of my home state made snake avoidance almost impossible. Once, a pygmy rattlesnake slithered into my work office after a hard rain. A who-knows-what kind of snake found its way to my bathroom after a similar storm. My most defining snake moment came early in life when a forearm-thick snake wrapped itself around my albino bunny's outside cage. The snake stared at poor Frosty. As I remembered it, Mom rushed next door. Our neighbor ran over with a shovel. I don't know what happened next. Mom and I stayed hidden inside. We asked no further questions.

As a Floridian, I should have made friends with these snakes. They, like snowbirds, loved our subtropical climate. There was just something deep inside that stopped me from befriending the reptiles. When I started to write about the Everglades pythons, people wanted to know why. If I couldn't even look at one online, then how could I go out and hunt them? I told them I wrote about issues that nagged or scared me as my own form of desensitization therapy. Apparently, I'm a masochist.

The python problem, like Florida problems in general, was man-made. The pythons found themselves in the state because people wanted to own them. Miami's port turned south Florida into the Epcot of exotics. Burmese pythons and their so-called objective beauty were staples of the pet trade. Between 1996 and 2006, a reported 99,000 of them were imported to the United States. People could buy these python hatchlings for sometimes as little as twenty dollars at reptile expos. The thing about a hatchling some people overlooked: it got bigger. The International Union for Conservation came to classify the species as vulnerable in its native range of Southeast Asia. The U.S. pet trade became regulated by laws such as the U.S. Endangered Species Act, the Convention on International Trade in Endangered Species (CITES), and various regional laws. In 2010, the State of Florida listed the Burmese python as a conditional species. Regular people could no longer get them for personal possession. Those who owned them could keep the animals with the proper license. Dealers, researchers, or public exhibitors could still apply for permits to import or own them.

The first reported wild python sighting in south Florida came in 1979. Along with pythons, the pet trade introduced about forty non-native snakes to Florida; those snakes included the Kenyan sand boa, green anaconda, whitelip python, monocled cobra, and tiger chicken snake. Some non-native species didn't harm the environment, but the FWC said others, like the Burmese python, became invasive because they caused harm to native species and posed a threat to human health. The story went that bad pet owners released the first pythons into the Everglades. The number of bad-pet-owner snakes may not have been enough to establish a population, but nature struck. Almost everyone I talked to pointed to 1992's Hurricane Andrew as the tipping point. The hurricane destroyed a python breeding center and released its snakes into the wild.

And the pythons liked to mate. I'd like to preemptively apologize for the mental image I'm about to give you, dear reader. Please no matter how curious you are, do not Google videos of snakes mating. You'll never be able to un-see it. Burmese pythons mate during orgies held in burrows dug out by gopher tortoises. A scientist described one of these sexy snake parties as "240 pounds of python in one hole in the ground. They just kept coming out, one after the other, and it just didn't stop." By 2000, these snake sex parties helped the pythons become an established species in the Everglades.

Early Everglades explorers like George Henry Preble were astonished by the land. Cypress, pine hummocks, and palmetto scrub dotted its landscape. He saw many streams with white sandy bottoms. His days were "rendered harmonious by the warblings of multitudes of feathered choristers and the night hideous with the splash of alligators, hooting of owls, and screamings of a variety of unquiet night-birds."

Preble and his men navigated the then uncharted area by canoes. The group stopped on islands to set up camp or slept in their vessels. They ate off the land. One day, an expedition member killed a rattlesnake with eight rattles. He skinned it and cooked the meat. "I partook of a bit," Preble wrote, "just to be able to say I had eaten rattlesnake."

I understood where Preble was coming from. I, too, wanted to eat a snake to say I'd done it. Before the Great Python Challenge, Jessica and I had visited Evan's Neighborhood Pizza in Fort Myers. The shop made national headlines with its pizza topped by python meat. Shop owner Evan Daniell opened his first pizza place in the 1980s at age eighteen. Evan went on to own six shops at separate times. His recent shop Neighborhood Pizza stood near the Caloosahatchee River. There was a big brouhaha about the overpopulation of pythons in the Everglades. He got to thinking he ought to put some on a pizza. It featured about two ounces of python meat on a 14-inch pizza. Evan didn't think they'd sell many, but he hoped people would talk about it. And talk about it they did. The python pizza was featured in publications like the *Huffington Post*, *New York Post*, and twice in *National Geographic*. "Generally, no one has tasted python," said Evan. "Rattlesnake, sure, but not python."

The Everglades Pizza cost forty-five dollars. Python, deep-fried frog legs, alligator, hog, and swamp cabbage (hearts of palm) topped the pizza. Evan bought Burmese python from a supplier in Vietnam. The supplier shipped the snake meat in dry ice to Florida. The meat arrived filleted in one-pound sections. Evan marinated it in Italian dressing then put some heat on it. He was able to buy other reptile meat closer to home. He had purchased gator meat and iguana, which I saw de-skinned and shrink-wrapped. There wasn't an authorized, local source for the python. People couldn't eat the Everglades pythons because of their high levels of mercury. There was no telling what they'd consumed out there. "I can't just go out and club a python and then serve it to you," he said. The shipped-in pythons had been farmed specifically for human consumption. He first bought the meat online for about sixty-five dollars a pound. He was then given a number to call.

I once knew a guy who knew a guy who sold roadkill—possum and raccoon. I'd never heard about exotic meat retailers. I discovered people can buy all kinds on the internet. Emu Hot Italian Sausages for $29.99, 2 pounds of Camel Andouille, and Beaver Burgers for $39.99 per pound. Less than a pound of lion steak went for $400 to $600. The exotic meat aspect had brought people into Evan's store. He sold two to five python pizzas a week. Friends ordered the pizza as a challenge to see who would and wouldn't eat it. "People want to experience it," he said. "They want to say they've done it."

As with the early explorer Preble, I wanted to say I'd done it. But I didn't want to actually do it. I imagined little pieces of snake somehow becoming fully formed in my stomach. The snake would then reassemble and eat me from the inside. I hated snakes, but I hated wasting money even more, and I had already made the trip to Fort Myers. I accepted my fate.

Jessica and I chose an outside table, and Evan's daughter brought us a metal platter with raw bits of alligator, frog legs, and skinny slices of python. These bits would get placed into a wood-fire pizza oven to make them edible. "People are pretty nervous about eating the pizza," she said, "but some people man up and do it."

About a half hour later, the python pizza stared at me.

The cooked gator looked like sausage, and the thick frog legs like chicken wings. Tiny pieces of shredded python meat sat atop the cheese. I psyched myself up and took a bite of the snake. It didn't have much flavor. It was tougher than chicken and chewy. Pythons were basically all muscle.

All participants in the Great Python Challenge were required to take online training and needed to pass a culminating quiz. Responsible beginners also underwent in-person FWC training. Before our hunt, Jessica and I spent a Saturday at the Loxahatchee National Wildlife Refuge. We trained with about fifteen other snake hunter wannabes. Two men sat on chairs near us. They showed each other cell-phone pictures of reptiles. No one in the group had seen a Burmese python in the wild, but south Florida offered plenty of other snakes to photograph. Jenny Novak, coordinator for the FWC's Python Patrol Program, greeted the room. "If you watch shows on pythons, you'd think we walk out of the house and trip over them here," she said. "But that's not the case."

The first week's hunters had handed over about forty snakes to the FWC. The year's top team would receive a grand prize of $5,000, and the biggest individual award was $3,500. The FWC created the Python Challenge as an effort to protect the Everglades habitat, and they were doing so by removing the invasive python. Scientists had tried various other methods to control the snake population. One of these methods deployed so-called Judas snakes. These snakes got caught, were tagged, and then released back into the wild and tracked (thus, selling their snake brethren out like Judas did Jesus). The scientists hoped to follow the pythons to gopher-hole sex parties. They would then eradicate those sinful snakes as well as their potential offspring. This pornographic method proved time-consuming and expensive. It was cheaper to wrangle up some hunters and let them roam the Everglades for a few weeks.

FWC's Jenny Novak told trainees if we caught a wild Burmese python and decided to kill it, we needed to use a shotgun or pistol with shotgun bullets. Jessica's gun permit hadn't been approved in time for her to buy a weapon before our trip, so this tip did not apply to us. Jessica still asked, "If you shoot the python, but it's not dead, can it still bite you?"

"Yes," Jenny said.

The snake's afterlife chemical reactions allowed it to bite from beyond the grave. Other python hunter injuries could include falling into water or tripping over roots. "Be aware of how your body reacts," said Jenny. "People can lose complete control of their bodies around the snakes." This loss of control could start at the beginning of the process with the snake hook—a golf club meets dental pick.

It could also happen halfway through the process with the hunter already in motion. People got tunnel vision. Jenny had physically moved people for their own safety during training. The worst thing to do was to stand spread-legs over a snake's head and freeze. The snake could rear up with fierce strength. "People don't want to think they're going to have that reaction," said Jenny, "but some people do."

I knew without a doubt I'd be one of those people who froze or lost complete control of my bodily functions, so I kept my distance when we moved outside to train with a live snake. One of the attendees asked me how I could write about pythons without at least touching one. I'd usually agree with this line of thought on participatory journalism, but I knew I couldn't handle it. I ignored his comment. I didn't need to get deep into my psychological makeup with someone who liked to hunt snakes for fun. As Jenny had said, I needed to be aware of my body and my physical reaction to snakes.

I watched the group line up to catch the 7-foot training python. Most of the trainees lived in Florida, but participants traveled from all over the country. They registered as individual hunters or teams of two to five people. "I've always loved snakes," said Brandon Robbins, thirty-four, from Dallas, Texas. Brandon planned to hunt for a couple of weeks, but he found out his fiancée was pregnant, so he had to cut the trip short. The "huge snake fan" had owned three ball pythons and two red tail constrictors. He'd never owned a Burmese python. "I don't want to deal with the attitude," he said. "The bigger the size, the more it will hiss. This snake is the biggest and the baddest."

One by one the trainees knelt and used a snake hook to get the python under control. This hook proved important. If a person reached in front of the snake and not behind it, the snake could bite a hand in an instant. The group clapped for each successful capture of the lethargic python.

Jessica waited for her turn. She didn't share my fear of snakes. Her former roommate had owned a ball python. I hadn't known this when I hung out there. I also didn't know it had escaped its cage. On moving, they discovered the runaway snake dead in a curtain. When Jessica's turn came, she took the snake hook in one hand and a snake bag in the other. "Don't feel bad if it comes to your turn and you forget everything we've told you," said Jenny. "It happens every training. We may shout at you to keep you safe."

Jessica straddled the python. Jenny advised the python catchers to keep their mouths closed. The snakes tended to fling poop and uric acid as a defense. Jessica, unfortunately, learned this the hard way. As she reached for the python, she became the snake's target for its unspeakable mixture of bodily fluids. It sprayed this concoction as an act of retaliation, I'm sure, because we'd eaten its namesake on a pizza.

Jessica let out a yell, but she stayed focused. She didn't forget what she'd learned, even though the snake made her smell like its insides. Jessica grabbed the python behind its jaw. She placed it in the bag. The crowd clapped. I'd never been prouder of her.

An FWC employee gave Jessica a snake bag for her successful completion of the training. She brought this bag out on our hike with Leo Sanchez and Tim Meyer in the southern Glades. Jessica also referred to herself as "snake woman" for the rest of our trip. She unexpectedly became invested in catching a wild snake of her own.

During the first Great Python Challenge, people had caught sixty-eight pythons. This number proved the highest number of them ever removed in the timeframe. Leo, a short man with buzzed hair, participated in the inaugural hunt. He wanted to do even better for this second Challenge. He moved to Florida from Nicaragua in 1983 and had lived in Miami ever since. The day he spotted his first wild python, he "fell and was face-to-face with it." Then he stood back up, turned, and fell again. "The snake turned around and was hissing at me," he said. "It came at me, and I took a chance and grabbed him on the head."

He also recounted one of the "best days" of his life when a 12-foot python almost bit off his nipple. "The bite felt like the strongest man in the world with a pair of pliers," he said. Although Leo looked wild-eyed when he told me this story, it offered me a strange comfort. I believed he'd protect me when a snake attacked. He'd throw himself in front of a python headed my way. He wouldn't do this because he cared about my safety. He would do it for the rush. At least I wouldn't be the one with a python hanging from my nipple.

Leo wore a GPS around his neck and a camouflaged backpack. His cell phone rang. He took a business call in the middle of the marsh. Python hunters could sell snakeskin for about fifty to one hundred dollars each to Brian Wood's All American Gator. He worked with alligators, iguanas, snakes, stingrays and other types of exotic leather. The hunters brought in snake hides, and Brian turned them into belts, wallets, purses, jackets, interiors of vehicles.

That was if the hunters could find a snake.

Three miles of hiking with Leo and Tim turned up no python sightings. I had avoided snakes my whole life, but I hoped to see something other than a snake shadow in the Everglades. A python's famous diamond-shaped blotches served as an excellent disguise. Their brown, puzzle-piece patterns blended in among the Everglades muted sawgrass palette. Even trained herpetologists could face difficulty spotting them in the grass. Leo had hunted for about four months before he grabbed his first wild python. Five years later, he counted almost sixty grabs to his name.

A group of buzzards sunned themselves as Leo again disappeared into the marsh. He came out empty-handed. "You just lost a point," Tim yelled to him. "You walked past a racer."

Tim kept a point tally as part of the hunt. His laid-back demeanor was a 180-degree turn from the bombastic Leo. He cared most about the chase. Birds soared above our heads, and Tim easily identified them. The native Floridian said he only read animal books as a kid. He had taken this knowledge to herpetological meetings. As a child, he sat in rooms with adult herpetologists. They looked through reptile slides together. The herp community got its name from herpetology, which is the scientific study of amphibians and reptiles. Herpers, like Tim, usually weren't degree-granted herpetologists, but they still knew a ton about reptiles. They sometimes helped scientists with data collection.

Tim mentioned Florida legends like Tim Friede and Bill Haast. He had met Bill at herpetological meetings. Before Bill died, he directed the Miami Serpentarium Laboratories. He also became a practitioner of venom farming. Pharmaceutical companies used snake venom to create, among other things, pain relievers. Bill injected himself weekly with the venom he extracted. He wanted to see if he could build up antibodies. He kept up his ritual for decades and lived to be one hundred years old. His wife told a newspaper he died of natural causes. Tim also mentioned Tim Friede, a guy "who took it to a whole 'nother level." "He takes bites from anything—black mambas and cobras," said Tim. "He's like an experiment, and they run tests on him."

The day inched to 57°F, and Leo wanted a break. We stopped at a bridge near an abandoned control pump. He took out a joint and asked me if I wanted a hit. I declined. A calm breeze blew. Leo said these hunts helped clear his mind and kept him out of trouble.

Some groups also used these hunts as a form of therapy. The Swamp Apes helped disabled veterans build camaraderie with each other. (I should note the Swamp Ape is a Florida legend, like an Everglades version of Bigfoot. YouTube has some convincing sightings of these Swamp Apes, known by some as skunk apes). The Swamp Apes' Tom Aycock told me he found the snake hunts a "great way to decompress." He served in the military for thirty-three years and counted almost twenty years of volunteer EMT experience. "Getting back out to nature and letting some endorphins run is refreshing stuff," Tom said. "And if we can get a snake that's always good, too." They took folks out in the field to hunt no matter the disability, even in motorized wheelchairs.

For Leo Sanchez, any day out in the Everglades was a good one. "This is my happy place," he said. "I love this shit, whether I catch a python or not." He told me he's by-the-books. He didn't "even own a gun" because he didn't want his permits revoked. "Out here you're literally on your own," he said. "I fear coming across a human more than a python." He then let me know he'd heard a guy had been shot and dumped somewhere near us. His python nipple-bite story had made me feel more at ease, but this story—or the way he told it— had the opposite effect.

Leo finished his cigarette break as an SUV drove up a dirt path barely big enough to fit it. Haley Hanson, a Penn State graduate student, stepped out of the vehicle. The blonde twenty-two-year-old wore khaki pants and balanced a snake hook over her shoulder. She stepped around a large puddle to approach us.

"Did you have any luck today?" asked Haley. She lived in Tampa and researched invasive species. Leo shook his head no. "They should be out, it's nice," he said. "Yesterday it was windy as hell, and they caught a six-footer." The two discussed their python-catching strategies. They couldn't be further apart in appearance, but they both had a love for pythons. "I'm a permitted hunter, and I get calls from the state," said Haley. "I wish I could be out here every day." Haley didn't talk to us for long. She wanted to get back to her hunt. She climbed into the SUV's passenger side, and the driver whisked her off to a different part of the Glades.

The snake hunters soon decided to call it quits. We turned around to head back home without a python. I hadn't seen a snake of any kind on our hike. Not even the racer Tim had pointed out to Leo. That was just how it went sometimes.

The snake hunters got quiet until an engine rumbled behind us.

Two weekend-warriors stood in the truck bed. The Briggle brothers had Fieldcraft knives holstered to their jeans. The wife of one of the brothers drove the truck. This family trio arrived in the Glades close to 9:00 a.m. They, unlike us, had caught two approximately 7-foot-long pythons. "I pulled it out and grabbed it by the head," said Matt Briggle, thirty-six, a south Florida resident. "The other Challenge we got nothing, so even seeing one would have been 100 percent better."

The brothers said they killed the snakes by a quick stab with an Ikigun—a handheld harpoon that administered a powerful spike. It was considered a humane way to kill snakes because it quickly obliterated the brain stem. Leo mumbled that he doubted the two brothers caught the snakes that day. One snake, maybe. But two seemed pushing it. Some hunters allegedly killed snakes outside of the allowed hours and then transported the snakes to the Glades for the Challenge. Leo walked past the brothers. He wasn't too happy about their snakes.

I studied the Briggle brothers. Snake blood glistened. If they had faked the snake deaths, then they'd done a convincing job. I hadn't seen the brothers catch the snakes, so I couldn't know how or when they'd caught them. But I did see two dead snakes on the truck bed. I began to work up the nerve to get a closer look. I didn't have much time to be scared. The brothers wanted to get the snakes to Challenge officials. I walked to the side of the truck. The dead snakes moved their bodies, dancer-like. I remembered that chemical reactions allowed even dead pythons to bite. I took a step back.

The hike had exhausted Jessica. She asked the Briggle brothers if they'd give her a ride back. They said sure. I don't know why we deemed it safe for her to go with these men we'd never met. Men who killed pythons to relax. Without much discussion, she hopped into the truck bed. She stood next to the still-moving snake bodies. The hunters offered me a ride, too, but I would always rather walk than sit next to snakes. My fear hadn't subsided, but I looked at the pythons' slick bodies in the sun and saw more than shadows.

REPTILE PEOPLE

A pet smuggler told me Arizona had spoiled him. He'd recently made a trip to the desert and found a bunch of snakes. He put about a hundred of them into one box and placed this nightmare in his car. He planned to sell his finds under market value to get rid of them. He could face felony charges if he got caught transporting these snakes into Florida. Laws forbid people from taking certain animals out of the wild or across state lines. "I didn't want to get in trouble bringing all that stuff back to Florida," he said. "I had so much stuff on me that I would have been locked up for sure."

The smuggler started to smell something odd in his car on the way back from Arizona. He figured one of the rattlesnakes had vomited. He stopped and opened the box in a Texas parking lot. "We were pulling rattlesnakes out, trying to figure out which one threw up," he said. "None of them had, so we put them all back in the box."

In Arizona, he'd also caught a Gila monster, a venomous lizard with a black body and yellow splotches. These lizards grew to around 2 feet and weighed about 5 pounds. Their poison wouldn't kill a person, but they still packed a mean bite. People could legally buy Gila monsters from breeders, but taking them out of the wild was a federal crime. The smuggler had hidden the Gila monster behind his backseat. The car got so hot the animal overheated and died.

"That was the smell," he said.

This story horrified me for many reasons, and even more so because he seemed proud of it. I began to question some of my life choices. I also questioned my safety. The smuggler told me he had a buyer lined up for the lizard. The animal's death cost him about a thousand dollars. The Gila monster fried, but the snakes survived. He called one of these Arizona reptiles his life's prized finds. He planned to sell the pink speckled rattlesnake for fifteen thousand dollars. "Tom Crutchfield spent his whole life trying to find that thing," he said. "I was out there for about an hour. Talk about luck."

Florida native Tom Crutchfield was an OG when it came to animal smuggling. He started smuggling in the 1970s and brought thousands upon thousands of exotic reptiles into the United States. He also makes an appearance in the first few minutes of Netflix's *Tiger King*.

The first time I got Tom on the phone, the sixty-nine-year-old lay in a south Florida hospital. A crocodile monitor had bitten him. The monitors reached up to 15 feet long and were considered one of the most dangerous lizards in the world. Tom kept two in his backyard. He had been bitten only three or four times in his more than sixty years of reptile handling. This monitor bite was his worst. The injury occurred at his compound in Homestead, Florida. He'd broken his own rules to separate a lizard fight when he entered an enclosure with no backup help. The female monitor gave him a "warning bite." "She could have easily taken my finger," he said. "I could have bled out if she tried to bite it off."

We chatted on the phone for a bit longer. I told him I wanted to hear his take on the invasive Burmese python situation. The pet trade he'd been so heavily involved in often got blamed for the Florida problem. Tom said if his upcoming surgery proved a success, I could visit him at his reptile farm. He kept alligators, venomous snakes, iguanas, turtles, and other reptiles. The compound wasn't open to the public, and, he said, it never would be. "I'm a little more than a guy who has snakes," he said, "like a lot more. You just need to Google me or something."

Born in 1949, Tom came into the world with "a genetic predisposition to love reptiles." The sixth-generation Floridian caught ring-necked snakes in his backyard as a kid. He kept these snakes in jars and tried to feed them cheese. He liked to read Charles Darwin and admired Theodore Roosevelt. The self-identified Florida Cracker grew up poor. His childhood home didn't have running water or indoor plumbing. Tom lacked creature comforts, but he never lacked creatures. He continued to catch snake after snake after snake. He sold some of these to the Ross Allen Reptile Institute in Silver Springs, Florida.

Ross opened his Reptile Institute in 1929 to showcase Florida's wild animal life. He caught rattlesnakes and alligators with his bare hands. In a promotional video from the 1960s, Ross and his fifteen-year-old son Tom tussled with a 20-foot anaconda. "With the anaconda securing two coils around Tom's legs," said the video's narrator, "Ross swims into the rescue." Ross marketed the land's wildness as an environmental fantasia. People wrestled alligators and performed in snake pits. His Institute became one of the most well-known wildlife attractions along with Panama City Beach's Snake-a-Torium and Orlando's Gatorland.

Ross had movie-star good looks and a genuine interest in science. During World War II, his operation extracted venom from around seventy-four thousand snakes. They provided "raw material for antivenom bought by the U.S. military." His reputation spread. Young snake men traveled to him for guidance. Tom Crutchfield worked for Ross during his teenage summers. Ross became a mentor and taught Tom "a lot, a lot, a lot."

Tom wanted to pursue science until his college professor told him there weren't many careers in herpetology. He dropped out of school and found a job in the plumbing department at Sears. He and his wife, Penny, saved money to travel. Like a true Florida love story, the two had met when she worked at the Snake-a-Torium. As a married couple, they visited the Caribbean to catch reptiles and spiders. The couple transported their finds to the states in suitcases or in Penny's purse. Tom started his first exotic reptile mail-order business in 1979. He named it Herpetofauna Incorporated. He later operated Tom Crutchfield's Reptile Enterprises, Inc. He sold to private collectors and certain zoos. He said those zoos dealt with him because they didn't want to undergo the long permit process. At his peak in the mid-eighties, Tom grossed close to $2 million a year from the animal trade. During this time, he liked to lift weights, drive Mercedes, and buy Rolexes.

A good part of his money also went to legal fees.

In 1995, Tom was convicted of smuggling endangered Fiji iguanas. This conviction came after a reversed and remanded court decision. The original case's prosecutor was Tom's previous customer. The prosecutor had "repeatedly and improperly attacked" the character of the defendants and their witnesses. For Tom's 1995 conviction, he received federal probation. He fled to Belize and spent time there in a prison before the country expelled him back to the United States in 1997. During this same time, the U.S. Fish and Wildlife Service launched Operation Chameleon, a five-year probe of the illegal reptile trade. The international investigation led to indictments, arrests, or prosecutions of people from the United States, Canada, Germany, the Netherlands, South Africa, Japan, Malaysia, and Hong Kong.

Operation Chameleon found Tom had conspired with two German nationals to smuggle Madagascar tree boas. He also smuggled ground boas, radiated tortoises, and spider tortoises. Those were protected species under the Convention on International Trade in Endangered Species of Wild Fauna and Flora (CITES). Tom had concealed the reptiles in suitcases and transported them on airplanes. In 2000, a court found he acquired other exotic turtles from a Japanese national. He acknowledged illegal activities involved in the smuggling of more than two hundred reptiles. The court sentenced him to thirty months for seven felony counts of conspiracy and smuggling. He also violated the Lacey Act. The act made it unlawful to "import, export, sell, acquire, or purchase fish, wildlife or plants that are taken, possessed, transported, or sold in violation."

People have called Tom a horrible person. He took animals from their natural habitats and sold them. He broke a bunch of laws, and people said he wasn't the nicest guy during his smuggling days. The first time I talked to him, he told me he'd retired from pet smuggling. An FWC spokesperson said he was in good standing with their organization. I wanted to interview him because he brought invasive species into the United States. I also wanted to interview him because I ran away from the things Tom had run toward.

Tom spent most of his retirement time breeding reptiles. He advertised them on Facebook. He sold an adult female monkey-tailed skink for $1,075, red iguanas for $375 each, and offered the 2017 Crutchfield crimsons on sale at $1,975 (only seven left). He also bred venomous snakes. He didn't sell those to strangers because "of idiots who sometimes buy them" and then post pictures online doing "stupid stuff" with the snakes. "I did a lot of illegal stuff, and I'm sorry I did some of it," he said. "I caused my family pain, and I'm sorry I brought bad publicity to the herp industry itself."

I wanted to see a part of the herp industry for myself, so I visited Repticon Tampa in 2019 and stood in line with reptile fans outside a convention hall. People held turtles in plastic containers. Lizards clung to their shirts. A man passed me with an orange-and-red snake hung around his neck like jewelry.

"Do you know what kind of snake that is?" a man behind me asked.

I didn't.

"It's a corn snake," he said. "They're good for your house because they eat rodents."

The first real Tampa Repticon took place ten years earlier. The expo bounced around locations but ended up at the Florida State Fairgrounds. As a child, I loved the State Fair's rides. They flung me to the sky and spun me around until I was weightless. Those rides made me feel nauseous as an adult, but I still liked the fair. I liked to eat elephant ears and all the fair food. I'd been to the fairgrounds before, but I'd never been to one of its expos.

The inside of the 40,000-square-foot Special Events Center looked like a job fair. At a booth near the entrance, kids got their face painted like Spiderman. Near them, a girl in a stroller pulled a plush purple fake-snake around her neck. A group took pictures of a man who held a black-and-white Argentine tegu as if it were a baby.

A spokesperson told me the expo reached a point where the vendors sold out early. These vendors included Dirty South Reptiles, King James Pythons, Premium Crickets, and Super Bad Reptiles. These vendors sold Asian vine snakes, crested geckos, brown house snakes, spotted turtles. Clear boxes held eastern chain kingsnakes, a Miami corn snake (female), Japanese rat snakes, south Florida yellow rat snakes. At one booth, snakes were identified like ice cream flavors: Lemon Blast, Butter, and Cinnamon. Ryan's Reptiles sold dart frogs for eighty dollars. A vendor sold two bunnies. Someone later told me those bunnies may have been snake food.

Takeout containers held a red-lipped alligator lizard, Cuban false anole, and an *Abronia deppii* (rare). A pair of sulphur water monitors went for four thousand dollars. "Oh my God, there's so many," someone said as she walked past DaVinci boas, a vendor who sold an all-white "super fire" boa for ten thousand dollars. This "super fire" was the most expensive snake I saw for sale, while the least expensive snake cost seventeen dollars.

The Repticon snakes looked sleepy. I asked one of the reptile breeders, an engineering student with a beard, why the snakes seemed so tired. His table sold colorful pythons. I assumed vendors fed them the previous night to keep them happy and sluggish. "We feed them about a week before," he said, "otherwise they might defecate in their containers." The engineering student said he enjoyed the process, but he had begun to scale back his operation. Breeding took time away from his studies. It took about three years to get a snake from baby to breeding size. The snakes at his booth curled up because they were cold. Earlier, in the day, they'd been more active. One had broken through the plastic container.

A vendor near the engineering student sold gargoyle geckos. The third-grade teacher didn't want me to use her name because of her job. "People at work have an easier time accepting that I'm gay than they do about the reptiles," she said. The teacher incorporated reptiles into her classroom. She said this helped students get over their fears. She had learned a lot about taking care of animals from the herp community. "There's also a camaraderie," she said. "I've had a very positive experience in the community."

Susan Barr had also found a place in the herp community. She walked around with a Patagonian mara named Jinxy the Jackalope. She'd brought the long-legged rodent to help educate people on why the cute animal didn't make a good pet. They were like a two-year-old on speed. Susan, fifty-eight, grew up in New Jersey. She worked in the Catskills and graduated from the New York School of Dog Grooming. She moved to Florida and opened a grooming shop in Spring Hill. Now, she boarded cats. "The money from my business fuels my desire to own a bunch of exotic animals," she said. "I have emus, alpacas, miniature donkeys, a whole bunch of animals in the backyard for the cats to watch."

Susan told me she was autistic and zeroed in on animals. They'd been an obsession since childhood. "I just find every single animal so interesting," she said. "You really don't get to know them until you own them." She attended Repticon Tampa the previous year, but she didn't interact with people. She had been shy, but this year Jinxy helped her open up. "After all these years," she said, "I've learned dog people are extroverts, cat people are introverts, bird people are masochists, and reptile people are my people."

The term "reptile person" might conjure up an image of a teenage goth with a hundred piercings, but people of all ages, socioeconomic brackets, and ethnicities walked around the expo. Official attendance numbers weren't released, but the two-day crowd probably would have sold out an almost-famous rock group's farewell tour concert. I was surprised by the number of kids there. I was even more surprised by how many of them held snakes. A young girl wore a black "snakes make me happy" T-shirt. A boy held a lizard dressed in a cowboy hat and dragon wings. I was jealous of them because I, still, never wanted to hold a reptile. The kids looked so cool with their lizards casually chilling on their shoulders.

Emma Dixon had first gone to Repticon Tampa at thirteen. She liked seeing the variety of animals because she didn't get to see them anywhere else in person. "I can look at all the pictures online," she said, "but actually being able to come here and experience all of them and sometimes hold them and learn about them is what I enjoy." The now eighteen-year-old loved reptiles and thought they got a bad rap. She said they embodied character and personality. They were more afraid of you than you should be of them. Emma didn't own any reptiles. Yet. "There's a long list of snakes, lizards, and geckos I want," she said. "I was seriously considering a spider today. The tarantulas are really pretty."

At a booth, I watched a grandma get a chameleon to walk on her shoulder. Her grandson bent down for it to step on his head. They laughed. The chameleon looked grumpy. A dad with two children bought a pack of frozen mice—a 25-pack of "fuzzies," sized 5–7 grams, for $27.50. They could also buy frozen rats—a 50-pack of pinkies (3–8 grams) for $62.50 and a 3-pack of "mammoth" (up to 1.3 pounds) for $22.50. Rihanna's "Please Don't Stop the Music" played somewhere on loudspeakers.

I stopped at the MR Reptiles table. Two women haggled over the price of some lizards. A scorpion crawled on one of the worker's hands. A nine-pound giant Suriname marine toad stared out of an aquarium.

"That's the biggest toad I've ever seen," I said.

"It's big," said part-time MR Reptiles employee Arne Haryn, "but some African toads get bigger."

Arne rocked surfer's hair and told me he'd grown up looking after frogs. They were one of the most difficult animals in the business to keep because of their sensitive skin. Arne preferred to work with invertebrates, mainly arachnids. He took care of tree spiders, orb weavers, and scorpions as well as centipedes and millipedes. One of his favorite aspects of his job was having the opportunity to ease people's fear of animals. At the expo, he let people hold a snake (I, of course, was not one of them).

Arne's mom had worked in a pet store that sold parrots, gibbons, dogs, cats, and monkeys (the nineties were a beautifully strange time for Florida pet stores). His mom regularly brought home an animal to see if he liked it. He started to attend Calusa Herp Society meetings in his early teens. These meetings brought together people of all ages and backgrounds. People gave talks on issues like preservation and invasive species. A member maintained the breeding grounds of the threatened-species eastern indigo snakes.

The Calusa Herp Society had about one hundred members. Arne hung around "the old-timers like Bill Love, Dick Bartlett, and Tom Crutchfield." I asked him about growing up around Tom. "In the animal business, Crutchfield is one of the most known people in the US and internationally," he said. "I heard about everything—the animal importation, the smuggling—but I never took it as him doing illegal things at the time. Everybody knew what was going on with him, but most people didn't judge him too harshly on it."

Arne stopped going to reptile meetings at twenty-one when he moved from Fort Myers to Bushnell, Florida. He worked at the area's Glades Herp Farm Inc., then known as the largest venomous dealer in the United States. One of its co-owners, Robert Keszey, starred in the Discovery Channel's *Swamp Brothers*. (I should note that in 2014, Robert was sentenced to a year in prison. He had a role in trafficking state and federally protected reptiles. After time served, he and his brother became part owners of the nonprofit organization Animal Crossings of Florida.) Arne had spent the latter part of his tenure at Glades Herp in sales. This led to a familiarity with Florida law. "You have to know every single law before you sell anything," he said. "It's hard at first to wrap your mind around how intricate it is—it's like trying to explain to someone how many stars are probably out there." Regulations varied at the federal, state, and county levels. "It's very intricate to make sure you're not selling illegally," he said. A seller might get a yes from the state, but a no from the county. These laws could change quietly and—according to folks in the community—arbitrarily. "The government should make it easier for people to be able to understand the laws," said Arne, "and there's a little more edge to the conversations in Florida."

Some people in the community blamed this edge on the media's narrative of reptiles like The Snake That's Eating Florida. Others blamed a communication breakdown between agencies and the community. Arne said some of the laws for reptile selling were unnecessary, but he liked most of them. "If someone was just able to go and be around a crocodile in an enclosure, you'd have a fatality," he said. "That's not only horrible for people getting killed, but it's also a blight on the business."

Arne thought back-in-the-day smugglers hadn't realized all they'd taken from other countries. "Now, we put money into the area and pay everyone who works down there when we export," he said. "Any of the conservationists, the native collectors, they get paid. It helps them out in the area." This made it harder for importers to bring in random shipments of venomous snakes to the country. "It's not the same now," he said. "People think differently about things."

I was told Florida reptile conventions had stricter regulations than some other states. States up North didn't necessarily have the same snake concerns. Escaped venomous snakes would most likely die in northern winters. Florida's weather would let them thrive. Floridians who wanted venomous snakes needed an adequate facility and stable finances. They also had to provide two letters of reference—at least one from a licensed FWC employee—and documentation of at least one thousand hours of handling. "I think there's more black-water events happening in Florida because of all the regulations," said Scott Wisneski, owner of Family Reptiles in Lakeland, Florida. "People want to own animals without having those types of permits. I don't agree with it, but I know people do it for the money."

Scott was born and raised in central Florida and lived there all his life. He owned a couple of snakes growing up, but he gave up reptiles when he got married. He had kids and worked as a police officer. One day, he took his then five-year-old daughter to a reptile show.

She asked him for a snake. Scott bought his daughter a little California king snake. "Call me a Care Bear," he said. Their daughter's expo snake was a gateway to their current business, Family Reptiles.

He and his wife ran a retail storefront as well as a large rodent and reptile farm. They bred bearded dragons and tortoises. But they were mostly into snakes. "There are people out there who don't own reptiles and hate anybody that does," he said. "I think people should respect people's right to own them just as we respect somebody's right to own a dog." Their family went to about forty-one reptile conventions a year and were a sponsor for Repticon Tampa. Their daughter, now in college, worked for them part-time. Scott's father did, too. During the breeding season, the family cared for somewhere between 1,500 and 2,500 reptiles. "We're all about regulation, and we want to make sure we take care of our state," said Scott. "We also want to make sure we're doing it legally, following steps, and doing it fairly."

Scott contributed to a campaign flyer I'd seen earlier at Repticon that read: "Don't Tread on My Reptiles. Today it is anacondas. Tomorrow it could be ball pythons!" This campaign had been a response to the Wildlife Commission's vote. They classified four snakes as prohibited species: the yellow anaconda, brown tree snake, Beni anaconda, and DeSchauensee's anaconda. The Commission's reasoning was to "proactively protect Florida from these invasive species becoming established in the state." This vote took the snakes out of the pet trade. It barred people from owning them for reasons other than research or education.

The decision to ban the reptiles came as a shock to Scott and the community. He and other supporters had organized activists and spokespeople. They attended meetings with the FWC. They had hoped to find a middle ground and get the snakes listed as a conditional species. A conditional classification would require people to get permits and training before ownership. "We thought that was going to happen," he said. The new statute banned the anacondas. People could no longer own them.

Scott said the media's Burmese python narratives had increased paranoia. He also said when an animal—like the yellow anaconda— got banned, it upped the black-market value. An animal with a hundred-dollar value inevitably increased to one thousand dollars. "Being a retired law enforcement officer," he said, "I can tell you I don't care where you go or what you do, there will be a criminal element involved."

The clean-cut family man railed against smuggling and the illegal pet trade. "You can't be taken seriously in your industry if all you're doing is violating laws," he said. "Every time someone gets arrested for doing something illegal in the reptile industry, it's a black eye. It looks bad on all of us." I asked Scott his thoughts on Tom Crutchfield. He laughed and said, "classic." "I'm not going to comment on Tom," he said, "but there is more of a professionalism today. What was done twenty, thirty, or forty years ago is just not what we're doing today."

Tom told me if he didn't die during his monitor-bite surgery, I could visit him in south Florida. He survived, so I drove to his compound in Homestead. He lived near an alligator farm and a place advertised as a monkey jungle. A friend said people moved to the area when they don't want to be found.

I passed an irrigated field and turned down a rocky road of baby-pool-sized potholes filled with topaz water. I pulled onto what I thought was Tom's property. Gallon jugs of bleach stood alongside two sheds. Near them was a long building with wood panels and white doors. Beyond some dirt and grass stood a small house painted aqua and pink. Peacocks hung out under a bougainvillea on the property. I didn't see anyone.

Tom had stopped answering my text messages on my drive to south Florida. I thought my pestering upset him. I remembered Tom's long rap sheet, but I was more worried that I'd driven onto someone else's property. Someone who was doing something worse than looking after giant snakes. A rooster crowed and Tom appeared. He greeted me with a handshake and some distrust. He wore a black Tommy Hilfiger T-shirt, shorts, and a Rolex. He looked sturdy, like Santa Claus with a sunburn. The surgery for the monitor bite turned his left pointer finger into a zombie appendage. There were too many stitches to count.

Next to Crutchfield stood Stacey Maltz, his much younger girlfriend. She held a 3-foot baby alligator named Squirt. Stacey said she dressed up the now-naked gator for holiday pictures. She made a point to tell me she took the costume off right after they got the shot. She'd met Crutchfield through Facebook and then in real life on her way to a cruise out of a Florida port. A few months after that, Tom offered her a job to help feed the animals. "I just packed my stuff up and came straight here," she said. The thirty-seven-year-old moved to Florida from her home state of Connecticut. There, she'd owned an iguana and a bearded dragon.

As we stood in his yard, Tom continued to look me up and down. I had never mentioned my fear of snakes to him. I had tried to play it cool in our previous phone conversations. He must have smelled my long-held reptile fear. I'd been at his farm only a brief time before he cut me down to size.

"None of these things want to hurt you," he said. "Reptiles are not your enemy. They hardly kill anyone. It's usually the person doing something really stupid, getting drunk and swimming with alligators, running from cops, jumping in a pond where they feed all the alligators at the farm." The Everglades pythons received so much attention because of a visceral reaction to the snakes. It was easy to paint them all as monsters. "A very large python might attack a human for food," said Tom before Stacey cut in to say, "but they won't attack just because."

"There are invasive plants that make the animals look like nothing," Tom continued. "The invasive plants change habitats more than the pythons do." The potato vine can cover a forest and kill it. The vines prevented photosynthesis. Brazil peppers can crowd out other plants. "The goddamn feral cats," he said, "are even worse than the pythons."

Rod Sadler, Tom's longtime friend, agreed. He hung out at the compound in a baseball hat and skull-emblazoned tank top. He'd met Tom twenty or twenty-five years earlier when he'd given Crutchfield a boa constrictor. The two remained in contact over the years. Tom taught him how to handle venomous snakes. "A cat is fuzzy, soft, cute, and you want to pet it," said Rod, "but in the wild, they kill thousands of birds." A Burmese python could eat and then not eat again for a while. A loose, feral cat predates every day; it could potentially prey on multiple birds in that time span. "Their impact is way more, but it's a kitty," said Rod. "If a person sees a snake or python or lizard it's a problem, but the cat is cute."

Tom gestured toward the baby gator Squirt. He planned to build a limestone pond with chairs in the water so he and Stacey could sit with the gator. They'd do that until it grew to about 10 or 12 feet in length.

"Do you see this alligator trying to bite?" he asked me. He pointed to the cuddly Squirt. "Normal alligators don't do this. This is after training. I mean this little alligator, if it wanted to, it could tear your finger completely off."

"He's beautiful," I said.

"Do you want to hold it?" he asked me.

"No," I said.

"You can hold it. It's not going to hurt you."

"I really don't want to hold it."

"Do you want to touch it?"

"No."

"It's really not going to hurt you at all."

"I don't want to have a reaction and accidentally throw it," I said.

"Why don't you just touch it? I'll talk to you while you do it."

Stacey held Squirt, and I touched a meaty part of its tail. "It can't get to you," said Tom. "Feel its skin. This is the part they use for leather. Now come look down the alligator's throat. See how you can't see anything. The epiglottis covers it."

Tom referred to Squirt as it, because the gator proved too small for him to stick his finger "up in it to tell" the sex. "Male alligators have enormous penises, but they're all inside," he said. "I hope it's a male, so it will get big." "It doesn't matter either way," Stacey said to Squirt. "I'll still love you no matter what."

Little insects flew around Squirt's mouth and eyes. It seemed pretty chill, but I still didn't want to hold it.

"You know what the difference is between fear and appreciation?" Tom asked me.

"No," I said.

"Knowledge," he said. "We're afraid of things we don't understand."

These types of quips ran throughout my conversations with Tom. He switched topics from alligator penises to Buddhist philosophy to climate change. He recited scientific names of reptiles like song lyrics. He had an almost encyclopedic knowledge of snakes and those who studied them.

He gave up his efforts to get me to hold Squirt and led me through a chain-link fence. One of the compound's previous owners allegedly ran cockfights out of it. He didn't agree with making animals fight, but the property's former use proved handy. It came with cages. He estimated that at any given time he kept around 1,500 reptiles on his property. I had arrived at his place a little late in the day, so most of his outside reptiles had started to get ready to sleep.

"I don't think of these as pets," he said. "I think of these as friends and things that I'm learning about."

Tom guided me by cages of iguanas that looked straight out of *Avatar*. He separated his current iguanas by their vibrant colors: yellow and teal. His "Crutchfield crimsons" were named after him because he created them. They had red patches and "super reds" completely turned red.

In south Florida, boring, green iguanas roamed feral. The previous winter, I'd read reports of stiff iguanas that fell frozen out of trees. Some people assumed the iguanas to be dead, but they weren't. One Floridian reportedly picked up a bunch of these frozen iguanas. He put them in his backseat. They started to thaw as the car warmed. The Lazarus reptiles caused an accident.

As with the Burmese pythons, those iguanas were invasive. They ate lots and lots of vegetation and left behind bacteria. Iguanas became such a big issue in south Florida that the FWC at one point encouraged landowners to remove them from their property. "People don't like the feral iguanas," said Tom. "They eat up their garden, but a lot of those plants are invasive, too."

Tom walked me to a cage about 8 feet tall. He took out two yellow iguanas. They wrapped their tails around his hand. I'd never seen anything like them. They looked surreal. Like aliens. In that moment, I realized I'd never see these iguanas again on this earth. Their colors came from bred recessive traits and didn't exist in nature. They couldn't. Their hues would make them targets. They'd be eaten and wouldn't survive predation.

Tom told me he received a full social security check, and these iguanas paid for everything else. Tom hatched about one hundred per year. He could sell them for anywhere between $1,000 and $25,000, depending on the color and rarity. A goalie from an NHL hockey team purchased one of his most expensive iguanas. "The lives of the animals are more important to me than the money," he said. "I don't keep as many as I can for a strictly commercial thing either. It's not that it's necessarily wrong, it's just not right for me."

Tom placed the gemstone iguanas back in their cage. He told me he wanted me to meet Bertha, a "20- or 21"-foot-reticulated python that weighed around 200 pounds. FWC caught Bertha about eight years earlier and brought her to Crutchfield. "Bertha just got bigger and bigger and bigger," he said. "I'll give it a home the rest of its life."

(A spokesperson for the FWC told me the organization "has placed reptiles at Tom Crutchfield's facility in past years. FWC places animals at licensed facilities with proper caging. Current licensing held by Crutchfield is in good standing with FWC, and there are no known issues with the facility at this time.")

Tom kept Bertha at the back of his property in a 16-by-12-foot habitat with a pool, trees, and a reinforced shelf for her to rest on. He said people sometimes kept these kinds of snakes in a cage only 10 feet long. He despised the practice. "I don't like to see big, big reptiles kept in really small quarters," he said. "That doesn't happen in the wild." He likened those smaller cages for big snakes to a human forced to live in a closet. "A lot of people in the herp community get mad at me for telling the truth," he said, "but I think I know what is right."

Tom instructed me to squat down in front of the big snake's cage. "Take this flashlight," he said, "and shine it under this thing." I did as I was told. I hoped for the best, which meant I hoped I wouldn't see Bertha. I shined the flashlight into a cave-like enclosure. I spotted the snake coiled up, thick as a palm tree. I looked for about five seconds before I handed back the flashlight.

"A python," Tom said, "sees the world differently than you do."

Bertha understood her surroundings through infrared heat sensors on her labial pits, the area between scales. The heat imprint of an animal told her its size. The snake was genetically programmed to think anything bigger than it would kill it. "Once you see the world how they see it," he said, "then you know how to act around them."

"I think that's my problem," I said.

"Your problem is that you're anthropomorphizing them and seeing them through the ape's standpoint," he said. "All we are—we're just fucking talking apes riding around on an organic spaceship. Nothing more, nothing less."

We turned away from Bertha and headed toward Tom's house. I'd seen the big snake and survived. I felt a little calmer as he led me again past the expensive iguanas. Instead of going into the house, he turned toward the long shed. The structure looked like a barn. The doors were marked by placards emblazoned with DANGER VENOM-OUS REPTILES. I only wanted to talk to Tom. I hadn't signed up to walk into a room designated by an all-caps placard.

"Now, remember," Tom said outside the Rattlesnake Room, "you don't have any experience with rattlesnake rooms. Normally, if you go into a rattlesnake room it's deafening because they're all afraid."

Tom didn't need to remind me I'd never been in a rattlesnake room because my body had already done that for me. I went cold. I couldn't envision what a rattlesnake room would look like. I had spent precious brainpower avoiding the scenario. Would they be in cages together? Would they be fighting? I wanted to tell Tom no thanks, but my journalistic instinct usually overrides my good sense. I followed him into the all-caps room.

I expected the rattlesnake room to sound something like ten thousand maracas. But the room was silent. Dead silent. He kept the snakes in small, stacked boxes reminiscent of filing cabinets. Tom estimated he housed a couple of hundred rattlesnakes in the Rattlesnake Room. He and his team milked snakes in this part of the shed twice a month to extract venom. This venom went to medicinal research.

I thought I might see a snake slither around Crutchfield's yard, or maybe I'd spot one in the rafters of his sheds. I didn't see any of this. Tom kept the snakes locked in cages as the law required him to do. He owned some of the rarest, most venomous snakes in the world. Glass cages contained snakes with demure names such as sand viper, Mangshan pitviper, monocled cobra, and king cobra. I knew these names because the law required him to mark each habitat. Tom owned an Arizona black rattlesnake, a Gaboon viper, and a rhinoceros viper with tiny horns on its head.

He also owned a snake he dubbed the "Purple People Eater."

Tom walked to the back of the room. He pointed at a rack and a clear box with Sharpie hearts on the front. It contained a sunset cobra.

"Here's a cobra we don't milk because it's so defensive," he said.

Tom held a snake hook in his right hand. He opened the box and jostled the snow-white cobra. The snake popped up as if attached to a spring. As if it waited all day for this moment. The snake lunged at Tom, but it stopped right before his body. The cobra then turned its back to the snake handler.

"He's scared to death," he said.

I was, too.

I stood speechless behind a cart with cleaning spray bottles on it near the door. The snake focused on Tom. Tom had handled venomous snakes for more than fifty years. He'd been bitten three times. Two bites occurred through a bag and the other because a snake smelled a rat he'd earlier handled. I rationalized the cobra would bite him before it came for me. It looked like they had a long-standing beef.

"The snake is not going to attack anybody; it's going to defend itself," he said. "Do you understand? When I tell you, venomous snakes don't attack people, they don't."

I did not understand, but *yes, sure I do, now please get that snake back in its box.*

"If a person gets bit by a rattlesnake," he said, "it's because the person stepped on it or fucked with it and the snake was afraid."

I couldn't be sure how much longer Tom's speech lasted—a few minutes or a few lifetimes. I was having something like an out-of-body experience. Tom turned his back to the cobra and looked me in my eyes. The cobra lunged again but stopped short of him.

"These are not demons," he said. "I know how to make them not afraid of me, so they won't bite me."

Tom broke his gaze from mine and turned back to the sunset cobra. "Everybody can't have these," he said. "You cannot allow the public to be at risk in any way. I take it seriously because I have to." He looked the cobra in the face. He put his hand in front of the snake and slowly waved at it. The snake immediately went back inside the box as if it were a magic trick.

Inside his house, Tom offered me vegan oatmeal cookies and an assortment of unsalted nuts. His walls displayed art he'd collected over the years and various pictures of snakes. A huge alligator head rested on the floor. I didn't ask whether it was real or fake.

Tom's office nook contained racks of books like *The Biology of Rattlesnakes* and *Venomous Reptiles & Their Toxins*. Photographers had shot his reptile collection for books. He'd worked on a field guide of big snakes with a world-renowned scientist. Tom may have dropped out of college, but journals cited his research on reticulated pythons. He also published academically. In 2016, he coauthored an article for

Herpetological Conservation and Biology titled "Conservation of the Endangered San Salvador Rock Iguanas (*Cyclura rileyi rileyi*): Population Estimation, Invasive Species Control, Translocation, and Headstarting." His coauthors included a biology professor, the director of the Center for Biodiversity and Conservation Studies, an executive director of a research center, and a provost.

Tom was a true Florida Man: someone who did something outlandish (smuggled endangered species), got arrested for it (several times), and became infamous (or, as he said, "Google me"). His story encapsulated the things people feared about Florida. That we were just down here breeding snakes, drinking beer, and wielding machetes. Those parts of his story may have been true, but there were also other parts of his story. He was a Florida Cracker boy who grew up to travel the world, cowrite books with scientists, and breed iguanas worth thousands of dollars. He helped raise money for conservation efforts and gave lectures on reptile education. "I've certainly never been an enemy to animals or earth," he said. "I've smuggled lots of animals, but I've never hurt any animal."

Tom smuggled animals in the seventies when the laws "weren't being enforced too much." He "wanted to go to these weird strange places all over the world" and find animals he'd never seen. "I wanted to get the cool shit nobody had," he said. "That was our big plan." He "wasn't against making money." The business took him from his lack-of-running-water beginnings to being able to buy Mercedes. He may have liked the cash, but he didn't like what smuggling did to his head. His behavior changed. It led to his divorce.

Tom acknowledged the role he and others played in bringing invasive species to Florida. But he believed people needed to be more concerned with a different kind of animal: the human being. He talked about his ideas for more gun control. He said he wanted more protections for women and the LGBTQ community (or as he put it: "Who gives a flying fuck what bathroom people want to use?").

The Burmese pythons had altered the ecosystem, but people had done more damage to the planet and each other. He talked about carbon negative production and habitat destruction. He gave an analogy of a guy who walked into his house with a hammer and knocked a couple of holes in his walls one day, then the next day broke the pipes, then the next day did even more damage until the house crumbled around him. "The earth is the only place like it in the fucking universe," he said. "We need to help it." He and his scientist friends feared climate change had reached an irreversible point. The damage could only be fixed, he said, through sustainability.

Tom said he hoped I understood the snakes a little bit more for what they were. That they weren't the "terrible, brainless" creatures I saw them as. "They're not monsters of God," he said. He began to tear up. "They're like us. They just see the world differently." He reiterated the snakes wouldn't bite me unless I stepped on one (or, as he said, "if a giant tried to step on you, you'd fucking bite him, too").

We attacked things we didn't understand. People attacked what scared us, animals and other people alike. "If we don't change this behavior," said Tom, "none of us have a real chance to survive." The snakes were afraid. I was afraid. We were all afraid.

And we needed to stop meeting our fear with fear.

A REVELATION

As a child, I was scared of many things—like snakes and ninjas—but I feared hell the most. I attended a Southern Baptist megachurch and prayed more times than I can count to accept Jesus Christ as my Savior. I was *very* into God. I didn't cuss or say the Lord's name in vain, and I learned to recite the most Bible verses of anyone I knew. I went to church camp during the summers and bought Christian music CDs because I was an out-and-proud-DC-Talk-loving Jesus Freak.

My church ran the K-12 school I attended. We took Bible class every day and went to chapel once a week. The school taught creationism, the belief that God created the world and evolution wasn't real. Fun Florida Fact: in the late 1920s, the state led the creationist movement as legislators nearly decided to outlaw science-based teaching in schools; campaigns by groups like the Bible Crusaders of America kept the flame going, and Florida, again, nearly passed legislation in 2008 that would have outlawed evolution instruction. My school debunked evolution with logic like, *if the Earth was older than 6,000 or so years, there'd be more dust on the moon.*

Every student signed a book-length code of conduct at the beginning of each school year. One of the school's handbooks stated: "Each student should be of highest moral character and be obedient to all Biblical principles including, but not limited to, prohibitions against fornication, drug use, alcohol use, pornography, and homosexuality." The school's administration considered dancing a sin because it promoted impure thoughts. Boys had to stand at least "six inches away" from girls. This rule wasn't exactly an issue for me, although during this time, I prayed it would be. I hoped God would replace my gay feelings with a deep and primal lust for women. I must have been in middle school when I saw an allegedly gay teacher removed by security. I remember men in black uniforms storming into the band room and taking him by the shoulders. I wanted to do something to stop them, but I stood still. I was a few years away from being able to understand my sexuality, but I saw something of myself in the teacher, and I didn't want to get dragged out with him.

Around this time, my family and I were always doing church stuff, which, as a Jesus Freak, I usually liked. For a vacation, my grandmother, whom I call Gramel, took me to Orlando's Bible-based theme park, The Holy Land Experience. Twice. Orlando is most known for its Disney theme parks, of which I am not the biggest fan. I may let a tear fall during *Mulan*, but I soured on the "Happiest Place on Earth" after I spent Christmas Day there. A million or so other people made the same decision that year, and I got food poisoning from a turkey leg. Disney may be Orlando's biggest theme park draw, but there are plenty of other themes to choose from, like Islands of Adventure, SeaWorld, and Machine Gun America. I haven't yet ridden a tank at Machine Gun America, but I have seen Jesus hung on a cross at the city's Holy Land Experience (HLE).

The real Holy Land sans "Experience" is a sacred place. It's roughly located between the Jordan River and the Mediterranean Sea. The Holy Land Experience brought this biblical landscape to central Florida. It opened in 2001, and the Jewish Defense League picketed its first day of operations. The park eventually attracted visitors, but still found itself in debt. In 2006, then governor Jeb Bush signed a law to grant a property-tax exemption to HLE and other nonprofits that "display biblical manuscripts or stage scenes from the Bible." The next year HLE's board sold the park for $37 million to Paul and Jan Crouch. The couple had helped cofound the very profitable Trinity Broadcasting Network (TBN).

Jan Crouch took HLE and made it her own. She loved glitz. She spent money on gospel-glamour. A poetic Yelp reviewer described Crouch's changes as "everything is coated in gold glitter and fake diamonds, like Jan Crouch got methed up, cleaned out Michaels, then went on a 72-hour BeDazzler binge." To me, this wasn't a critique of HLE's aesthetic but high praise. HLE's TV commercials and cosmetic improvements finally drew a crowd. It started to become as profitable as a Bible-based theme park with no rides in Orlando could be. Visitors weren't able to go on roller coasters, but they could putt-putt golf balls at Goliath's head. The park cut back on its accoutrements after Jan died in 2016. They auctioned off a lot of her purchases in a large estate sale, an event I'll forever be crushed I missed. Post-Jan HLE reverted to its less fabulous, more historically accurate beginnings. They wanted the park to look like the Holy Land of biblical days, and the park focused efforts on their Scripture-based theatrical productions.

One of HLE's productions was a passion play. These performances re-created the crucifixion story. They can be intense. It's stressful to see a man—even an actor—get whipped to a bloody pulp and then hammered to a cross. My favorite Yelp-er from earlier described HLE's version as "a 75-minute orgy of blood and sequins that feels like the bastard child of Bob Mackie, Bob Fosse and Jim and Tammy Faye Bakker." This all took place in a massive gold and white coliseum easily spotted from the interstate. The building's exterior looked like a gaudy version of an amphitheater. The inside was even better. The park must have funneled the money it saved on roller coasters into its sound system. It was massive and worthy of a pop star's Vegas residency.

The last time I went—in my late-twenties with Gramel and my younger brother John—a huge LED screen formed the main stage backdrop. Two smaller stages ascended from the middle. I approached the passion play in a very I'm-on-vacation way and focused more on my phone until a park employee approached me. I feared this woman wanted me to go onstage for audience participation— my least favorite form of participation. *Did she recognize me as gay and think I needed prayer?* I decided to avoid eye contact with the woman at all costs. "You need to turn off your cell phone," she said. "They can affect the lighting cues." I slumped in my seat, embarrassed. I turned my full attention to the show.

A passion play re-creates the life of Jesus. This one added in a few marketplace jokes like "lettuce rejoice" and "isn't that grape." Actor-Jesus walked through the crowd and touched people on their ailing body parts. "Raise your hand if you have arthritis or ulcers," he said. "God can heal lung damage, even lung cancer—all types of cancer will fall into submission. Nerves that can't grow will now grow." The narrative then followed a familiar arc, one that gave me anxiety because I knew the impending gore. When actor-Judas betrayed actor-Jesus, John put his head in the neck opening of his shirt. He leaned on my shoulder and cried. I started to regret the decision to bring John to the play. Kids were in tears all around me. John had taken a selfie with actor-Jesus earlier. Now, he was watching him hang on a cross. A few minutes later, Jesus resurrected to fight Satan. John wiped his face. "This is awesome," he said. *Rocky*'s "Eye of the Tiger" blasted from the expensive sound system.

I had performed to this song years earlier when I joined the karate team of my church school's youth group. We fought for Christ and ministered to kids in Philadelphia, California, and Jamaica. I never got to be Jesus, but I did get to play an angel. In my angel-play years, I also gave other kinds of performances: I lowered my voice, dated a few girls. I wanted to follow Jesus, but it seemed like most people around me believed a gay person couldn't. I had been told there was no such thing as a gay Christian because all gay people were damned to hell for who they loved.

A Florida street preacher more recently reminded me of my impending trip to hell. More precisely, his sign read: *Warning: All homos will burn like faggots in hell! FAG-GOT/faget—a bundle of sticks or twigs bound together to be burned or used as fuel (Webster's 1813 OED Dictionary).* The street preacher and his crew took up residency in Ybor City, a section of east Tampa. Another Fun Florida Fact: Ybor City, once known for its cigar factories, was a center of radical politics in the early 1900s; Cubans, Spaniards, Italians, and other immigrants circulated writing on Marxism and anarchism to organize against their bosses. I'd mostly experienced the party life of Ybor City—a section of it looks like a version of Bourbon Street, full of bars and clubs.

This area attracted partygoers from post–punk rockers to hip-hop heads. It also drew anti-LGBTQ street preachers. They congregated in the neighborhood's gay district, known locally as GaYBOR. I don't necessarily like calling these men preachers because they do more yelling than preaching, but I will use the term since they identified as such. A group of them had "preached" in Ybor for at least a year and a half by the time I showed up to cover the LGBTQ counterpro-test organized by university students. But, as a journalist, I couldn't cover the protestors without at least trying to talk to the preachers.

I stood near five of them in front of my favorite convenience store, 7-Eleven. Anyone who has ever been to a Pride parade has probably seen similar groups. They're almost always men and shout Bible verses mixed with slurs. I watched one of the Ybor preachers point at a man and shout, "You're going to hell" as if it were a normal greeting. I tried to brush him off, but for a large chunk of my life, I had believed what he said to be true. A lot of church gays have thought the same thing. A lot of us prayed to be straight, and some of us took more drastic steps—forced into conversion therapy, sometimes referred to as sexual orientation change efforts.

In 2017, the City of Tampa passed an ordinance to ban conversion therapy for minors. At the time, it had been outlawed in states like California, New Jersey, Oregon, Illinois, and Vermont. President Obama had criticized the practice. A paper coauthored by a group of doctors listed the ethical issues as, in part, "breaches of confidentiality," "improper pressure placed on patients," "indiscriminate use of treatment," and "shameful internalizations that may induce or worsen depression." By the time Tampa voted on the ban, Exodus International, which was the nation's largest ex-gay group and based in Orlando, had been shut down by its president, who wrote he changed his mind and "chose to believe the truth about God—that he is indeed a God of love and grace." The Tampa City Council found "overwhelming research" that these conversion efforts posed "critical health risks." They passed an ordinance to fine first-time offenses at one thousand dollars and second-time offenses at five thousand dollars. The ordinance became law four days after it passed. The City was sued over the decision. A Christian ministry and a licensed marriage therapist alleged the City had overstepped its bounds in the regulation of health-care professions. The plaintiffs also cited a violation of free speech because of the talking aspect of the "therapy." The therapist who sued Tampa said he doesn't try to turn his clients straight but to help them "identify with their masculinity." This case went to a federal court, and a judge overturned the ban, in part, because it encroached on health-care law. The case had reached a high court, so the decision extended to the entirety of Florida, and it's currently legal for minors to undergo conversion therapy.

In Tampa's Ybor City, I stood next to a seventeen-year-old I'll call Tom. The high school junior had to get home by his Friday-night curfew, but he felt compelled to support his community. "I thought it right for me to represent those of us who are a bit younger," he said, "and give us a little bit of a voice." One of the street preachers stared at us. He had a buzzed haircut and wore a "Jesus Saved You from Hell" T-shirt. I hoped to never meet him on a street somewhere because of his eyes. They looked dead, like the life had been drained out of them. Next to him was another protester, a man with a bull-horn sporting a sticker with a line crossing out the word HOMO.

One of these preachers, Carl Junstron, sixty-one, took a brief pause from his crusade to talk to me. He told me he'd come out to Ybor to preach God's requirements for heaven and hell. Carl had piercing blue eyes and seemed to find it difficult to look at me with them. He attended a Baptist church, like the church I'd grown up in, but his crew didn't all identify with the same denomination. He said he wanted a civil discussion, and the signs—such as "homos will burn like faggots in hell"—spoke to God's wrath. "They need to repent from their sins," he said, "and turn to God." Another street preacher, Dan, who preferred not to give me his last name, had taken the night off work to disciple. He called the other men broth-ers. The thirty-five-year-old told me his group targeted the LGBTQ community because its members were a "wicked thing" and a "real attack on our children." "It used to be you'd worry about your daugh-ters getting raped," he said, "but now I'm more worried about my son getting raped than my daughter."

These statements gave me pause, but I'm used to people saying intense things to me when I'm reporting. I wanted to better under-stand these street preachers' fear. Why were they so scared of the gays? The preachers allegedly wanted to create a dialogue, and I tried to do that with them. This group, though, didn't much want to talk to me. They preferred to chant and yell and, sometimes, sing.

Most gay folks ignore these street preachers or take a selfie in front of their signs and keep it moving. But Donald Trump's election changed things for some in the Tampa community. Days after his presidential win, a small group of activists decided to counterpro-test the street preachers. Cofounder Aaron Muñoz said about six or eight people initially showed up with rainbow flags. Over the next few months, their group grew to twenty, then fifty, and sometimes more than one hundred people came out on Fridays for the "Wall of Love." "If it wasn't for the students showing up, it still might be a group of twenty people," said Aaron. "Students are really what made this a movement." Ashley, twenty-seven, and Ysabel, twenty-four, made the Wall of Love their date night. Community organizer Dayna Lazarus told me about another young couple who attended the University of South Florida (USF). The couple hadn't before seen an LGBTQ presence in the city. One guy was on the verge of tears when he saw the Wall of Love. He had felt encouraged to participate.

The Tampa Bay area is one of Florida's higher-education hot spots. It's home to two universities and several colleges as well as community colleges. These campuses mirror the area's urban sprawl, stretched across many miles and cities. USF has four campuses located hours away from each other. I was told student movements could find it difficult to gain traction. One student, Sarah Zaharako, twenty, heard about the Wall of Love through Facebook. The weekly protest provided an opportunity for activism she struggled to find on the USF campus. She and other students had taken strategies from the Wall of Love back to campus, confronting the street preachers who showed up there in a "repent sinners" truck.

Still, the main clash kept happening in Ybor. The ideological battle—for souls, the sidewalk—continued through bullhorns past midnight. Both sides shouted as clubgoers scrolled through their phones and waited to dance with their friends. The Wall of Love had grown to the point that people noticed them before the street preachers: Carl, Dan, and the rest. They stayed until nearly 1:00 a.m., and then, as uniformly as they came, the street preachers packed up and left. They planned to be back the next week, but so, too, did the Wall of Love crew.

I may have tried to hide my sexuality in high school, but I did get to sing a love song to my first gay crush in front of the student body. I'd been told my whole life to use my voice as an instrument for God, so I auditioned for the spring theater production. Our school had put on popular shows like *Godspell*, but the year I auditioned we performed the little-known *Way Out West in a Dress*. I suspect none of the administration had read the script. They gave the green light to a show that's basically about situational drag queens. Two gruff men inherit a salon, which they first mishear as "saloon." They think only women can own salons. They decide to disguise themselves by cross-dressing. I tried out for the lead drag queen, but the director passed over me. The role required a French accent I couldn't do and notes my post-puberty voice wouldn't allow.

My disappointment at not getting the lead didn't last long because it went to Frank, as I'll call him. Frank sang in the praise band, a high spot in the Christian teenage hierarchy. The director cast me as the bad guy named "Colt Revolver." I now see the irony of a gay student cast as the bad guy. Colt growls throughout the play and falls in love with Frank's cross-dressing character. He sings one solo, a love song to Frank, who Colt still thinks is a woman. On the show's opening night, I wore black jeans, a cowboy hat, and boots. I belted out my character's love in my best attempt at a "Western" accent. I couldn't tell Frank I had a crush on him in real life, but I could sing it to him through poorly executed lyrics. I professed my feelings in front of a room full of people who had taught me I'd be going to hell for liking boys.

For years, I'd hesitated to reconnect with people from my time as a high school student. I wanted to keep that part of my church past tucked away, but the Ybor City protestors made me think about my former life as a church-kid. A former youth leader, whom I'll call Travis, had been messaging with me on Facebook for about a year. I gathered from his messages that he, too, was gay. I decided I wanted to talk to someone who'd also grown up gay in my church—I wanted to see if I could somehow fit into the congregation.

We met for coffee on a rainy day. It'd been over ten years since I'd seen him, so he caught me up on his life. He'd left Florida to join the army after high school, then moved back to become a police officer near my hometown. I told him the best version of my career prospects at the time: *I have no idea what I'm doing with my life*. After the small talk, I asked about religion. "Do you still talk to anyone from the church?" I asked. "I haven't kept in contact with anyone."

I had distanced myself from the church, but Travis handled things much differently. He kept in contact with many people from the youth group. He had even stayed close to the pastor. I felt jealous. He seemed pretty chill about our past, but he did go on a tangent about how it's weird people focus so much on homosexuality. He said it isn't as explicitly frowned upon in the Bible like divorce or adultery. "It really doesn't even say anything about being gay in the Bible," he said.

In college, I took a "Literature of the Bible" course in which I re-read the Bible as a text. The class made me realize I'd internalized interpretations of the text from pastors instead of reading the actual words. When I looked at the stories outside of a religious context, I understood the Bible's morality to be a bit more fluid. My new look at the Bible led me to talk to theologians and Bible scholars. They seemed adamant that homosexuality would not send me to eternal damnation. I could then intellectually separate my faith from the church as an institution. Throughout this whole process, I still *felt* like a Christian. I never questioned my belief in God.

The rain fell harder, so Travis and I moved our chairs closer to the building. He'd stayed in the know with all the church people. There were "like ten people" from our church who were gay. Our conversation turned to my former high school. Travis had attended it for about six months before he decided he couldn't handle it. "That school's too sheltered," he said. "There's no interaction with any diverse communities." He told me about the time he happened upon a gay pride parade during one of our "urban youth" ministries. He told me about his youth group crush—a tall, lanky guy with freckles.

I had been nervous to reconnect with Travis, but I was glad I did. I hadn't realized how much I needed to tell someone else the full story. I hadn't realized I needed to hear someone say, *yeah, that happened, and I was there, too.*

I didn't think I'd ever feel comfortable attending my hometown church in Largo like Travis did. The church had posted an "Open Letter" after the Supreme Court ruled in favor of marriage equality. The Facebook post said the church "cannot and will not affirm the moral acceptability of homosexual behavior." (I asked Gramel if she'd attend my potential, theoretical gay wedding. She said, "Sure, if I'm still alive by the time you decide to get into a relationship. I don't plan to live forever.") Church had been a huge part of my life, and there were still parts—the stories, the singing—that I missed and loved, that reminded me of my family. So, when I moved back to Orlando, I decided to go to the city's gay church, the Joy Metropolitan Community Church (MCC).

A defrocked gay minister founded the MCC denomination in 1968. He held its first church service at his home in Los Angeles. He'd taken out an ad in a gay magazine, and twelve people showed up the first week, then thirteen the next, and fifteen the next until they needed their own building in the early seventies. The founder called himself a "liberal evangelical," and the denomination preached inclusivity around "issues of race, gender, sexual orientation, economics, climate change, aging, and global human rights." These churches welcome people of all religious stripes from Catholics to atheists and everything in between. In 2020, MCC counted nearly 43,000 members in almost three hundred congregations around the globe. Florida has the most MCCs of any state in the country at nineteen in cities like Key West, Jacksonville, St. Petersburg, and Sarasota. California has the next-most MCCs at fourteen, then Texas with thirteen of its own. I'd heard Joy MCC called the gay church, but the inclusivity extended past the LGBTQ community. They often had a presence at events like the MLK March or immigration rallies.

I rolled into my first Joy MCC service a bit late to avoid the pre-service chitchat. I wanted to feel out the congregation before I made any commitments. The Orlando church formed in 1979, and their building was much smaller than the mini-amphitheater of my childhood church, but it felt inviting. Stained glass windows let in sunlight. A series of doors stood in a row near the pastor; each of the doors was painted a color of the rainbow. I spotted a couple who wore matching purple shirts with glittery crosses on the back. The music director started to play an upbeat, almost bluesy rendition of a song about God's love. Reverend Stanley Ramos approached the microphone to say a prayer in Spanish. He led a Spanish-speaking service and prayer group on weekdays. Then, Senior Pastor Reverend Terri Steed Pierce took the pulpit to give a sermon on equity.

Reverend Terri first attended a Southern Baptist church at two weeks old. Her father was an alcoholic, so she learned to create a different kind of life through the congregation. She knew herself to be Christian before she knew herself as gay. She had memorized Bible verses, participated in church youth activities, and felt called to ministry at a young age in the early 1980s, but women weren't allowed to preach in most Baptist churches. The convention's reasoning went, *women were last created but first to sin.* She figured she might not be able to preach, but she would eventually be able to teach. Like a good

Baptist, she still attended a Baptist college. After graduation, she received a full scholarship to attend seminary.

During her first day at seminary, a guy walked up to her and said, *you're not here because you want to preach, right.* She learned early on that seminary would be a volatile place for her as a woman. Historically, the Southern Baptist church hasn't been the friendliest place for women, the LGBTQ community, or people of color. The Southern Baptist Convention was created to support slavery in 1845 (the same year Florida became a slave state). The church used verses from the Bible to argue for enslavement as a biblically condoned practice. "When I heard that, I looked around, like, who else is offended," said Reverend Terri, "but everyone was just sitting there."

She eventually fell in love with another seminary student—a woman she'd gone to high school with but hadn't known well. She struggled with the decision to come out but told a handful of people about her newfound love. "That was a terrible idea," she said. "That was the last straw, I mean, I didn't think I had much else going for me in the church." She attended a Baptist service shortly after this realization and sat down in her regular pew. She immediately felt the "biggest sense of peace" pass over her. "I knew me and God were okay," she said. "So that meant I was okay."

The Baptists still wouldn't let women preach, so Reverend Terri took a postseminary job at an optometry group. She began to compartmentalize herself. There was a version of her at home with her parents, one at church, and one with her partner. She went in and out of closet doors all day. She went to church services but didn't get involved in activities, even though she had loved them as a kid. After a while, the partner she'd met in seminary began to attend a gay-affirming congregation. One day, they went together. "I walked in and I just knew I was home," said Reverend Terri. "It was cathartic. These are my people." MCCs didn't have the same gender restrictions on who could preach, so she finally became ordained. A minister asked her to apply for the senior position at Joy MCC in Orlando. "There are more and more churches accepting us," she said. "It's a beautiful thing."

Reverend Terri told me some churches still used the Old Testament's Leviticus to keep out the gays. The verse I've heard most attributed to the *gays-will-burn* mentality is Leviticus 18:22: "You shall not lie with a man as one does with a woman. It is an abomination."

The whole eternal fate of the LGBTQ community hinged on these two sentences. I'd like to point out the next chapter of Leviticus lists a bunch of "decrees." These include: "Do not wear clothing woven of two kinds of material" and "Do not cut the hair at the sides of your head or clip off the edges of your beard." If a guy is a hipster who wears any type of polyester blend, then he's screwed. The Lord also decrees in Leviticus to "stand up in the presence of the aged, show respect for the elderly and revere your God." This verse doesn't bode well for those who live in cities with public transit as I've seen many people fail to give up their seats to anyone during rush hour.

There are a handful of other verses people sometimes point to, but the Leviticus verse is the headliner. I have to say Leviticus is a weird book to condemn a whole group of people, especially because it's in the Old Testament. A few denominations say those decrees went out the window when Jesus showed up. He chilled with all types of folks, including prostitutes and thieves. He turned water into wine to keep the party going at a wedding. He also had long hair and a beard. All I'm saying is *some* people *might* choose portions of the Bible to suit their viewpoints, and these viewpoints can sometimes do more harm than good.

Reverend Terri's niece Megan—like so many other gay Christians—had grown up in the church and struggled with sexual orientation. "The church had told me I was sinful," she said, "and I knew how the people I love would react to me being gay." As an undergraduate, Megan had fallen in love with a woman but then unceremoniously called it off. She couldn't reconcile being a lesbian with her Christian beliefs. She'd seen how some of her family members turned against her aunt for being gay and worried they would do the same to her if she came out. One day, Megan took a drive and intended to end her life, but something stopped her. She, like her aunt had years earlier, felt embraced by God in the dark hour.

Megan decided to take an internship at Joy MCC the summer before she went to seminary. Her internship at Joy MCC caused an unexpected consequence. Her father caught wind of the news. He was conservative and didn't agree with Megan working at the gay church. He asked if she wanted to work there because she was gay. Megan had thought—as many of us have—that she could keep her sexuality hidden for a little while longer. But her father asked her point-blank, and she didn't want to lie. She came out to him. He then called her an abomination and started to recite Scripture. Megan, who had majored in religion, stood her ground even though she felt hurt and shattered by the experience.

Joy MCC helped Megan heal after coming out, and the church became a haven for her, especially during her summer internship. She planned to tell a version of her coming-out story during a sermon at Joy MCC on Sunday June 12, 2016. That Sunday, the world woke to news of the Pulse shooting. A gunman had killed forty-nine people on Latin Night at the club. This club had been more than just a place to buy drinks and flirt. Early on in my undergrad career, Pulse had been a part of my regular going-out rotation; some of Florida's best drag queens performed there, and you could count on the DJ to play good music. Pulse, and other predominantly gay places, became opportunities for us to figure things out—who we were, how we wanted others to see us. I hadn't visited Orlando much after the subsequent joint funeral of my close friend Drew and his boyfriend, Juan, who'd died in the Pulse tragedy. I thought I needed some space from the city, but I had come back to teach at the University of Central Florida (UCF), in part, because I needed the community. On days I taught, I'd often walk by the campus mural of Drew and Juan painted on the university's Student Union building.

The Pulse tragedy took place about a mile and a half away from Joy MCC. The church immediately mobilized and tried to be of help. Joy MCC's Reverend Stanley Ramos learned about the shooting from his place in Atlanta. He had moved from Orlando to attend seminary at Emory. The news made Stanley's hair stand up. He booked the first available flight to Florida. Stanley had felt called to ministry early on, but he knew he'd need to stay in the closet to do so. "Being gay in the Puerto Rican community could be challenging," he said, "both in and outside the church." Stanley struggled with his decision but came out in the nineties and all but gave up on ministry. He earned a graduate degree in social work and then worked as a community organizer and a private practitioner. He'd never thought a gay church possible, and his life changed when he walked into Joy MCC. MCCs required pastors to graduate from seminary, so, in his fifties, Stanley gave up his professorial job at UCF to go back to school. He couldn't find a seminary in Orlando; they were all too conservative. He would have had to go back in the closet and even sign a paper denying his sexual orientation. Stanley had worked hard to live as an out gay man, so he packed up and moved to Atlanta to attend a pro-LGBTQ seminary.

After he found out about Pulse, he quickly got back to Orlando to help at the front lines. He joined other social workers, many of whom he'd taught during his decade-plus at UCF. They all hugged and cried together. Then they made a prayer circle. Orlando's response to Pulse opened his eyes to the intersectional struggles of the Latinx community in the LGBTQ world. "I kept seeing the lack of representation of brown and black people," he said. "There's one oppression with the LGBT community and another when you see the whiteness of it." He felt challenged to speak up for his communities and to become an even louder voice. Joy MCC's roots in liberation theology allowed him to connect pastoral work to activism. "Our voices must be raised to bring up social issues," he said. "I'm more political now."

Joy MCC responded to Pulse with activism and open arms. They advocated for the community. They showed what a church could be. In the aftermath of Pulse, people seemingly wanted to erase years of certain denominations' anti-LGBTQ rhetoric. Not even a week after Pulse, a national publication ran the headline "Orlando Massacre Brings Together Christians and Gay Community." Reverend Terri felt otherwise. Joy MCC had been "an afterthought" in most of the post-Pulse conversations. "They prayed for use because they felt sorry for us," she said. "And it felt hypocritical."

Longtime Joy MCC member Marlyn Moir said a lot of people still couldn't understand that a person could be a gay Christian. "We're not freaks," she said. Music ran in Marlyn's family, and the native Floridian performed in big tent church revivals with her siblings. One of the best places to sing in public is during a church service. A good worship leader will call voices "instruments of God" no matter if off-key, a descriptor I'm specifically applying to my own voice as Marlyn is an actual singer. Marlyn had also grown up being taught gays were damned to hell, but she soon came to terms with her sexuality when she fell for the daughter of a Southern Baptist minister. "If God made me, then there's nothing wrong with me," she said. The two women met in their twenties and played guitars together. Their relationship blossomed during the eighties in conservative

DeLand, Florida. I could barely believe it when Marlyn said this, but the Southern Baptist minister accepted their relationship.

Marlyn first attended Joy MCC in 1997. Currently, she served as the church's vice moderator; this basically meant she ensured policy and procedures. She lived in DeLand and made the 50-mile commute to Orlando, which sometimes took nearly two and a half hours depending on traffic. She worried about the church's future—how it would attract and keep the congregation's younger members. Pew Research found a widening gap in church attendance between baby boomers and millennials, who affiliate less often with religion in general. Strict fundamentalist views may have turned off younger people. All kinds of people—not just those in the LGBTQ community—have been told church wasn't a place for them. "That's what drives people away from church," said Marlyn. "We need to listen to the young people."

Brian Wood noticed Joy MCC's congregation skewed older and wanted to help. The thirty-three-year-old grew up in Wisconsin and visited Disney on his first college spring break. He saw a thriving gay community in Orlando that had been missing in his part of Wisconsin, so he dropped out of college and moved to Florida. Brian got a job as a stripper at Pulse. He worked there for nine years as a bartender and eventually as the general manager. He then transitioned from his bar job to become a property manager, which he called "divine intervention" as it meant he wasn't at Pulse during the tragedy. Still, he spiraled after the shooting. He'd spent nearly a decade of his life at the club, and he turned to drugs and alcohol to cope with the great loss. Brian eventually began to live a sober life and went to Joy MCC with his friend. "The church was like instant family," he said. "It started to build my faith." Brian began to co-organize a Young Adult Ministry (YAS!). Group members ranged from eighteen-year-olds to people in their thirties. They sometimes discussed church stuff but mostly talked about their lives and ways to support each other.

During the COVID-19 pandemic, Joy MCC moved its services to digital platforms. They conducted Bible study, YAS! Meetups, and prayer on video conferencing apps like Zoom. Preaching to an empty room at first proved difficult for Senior Pastor Reverend Terri. She feeds off a room's energy. She likes to use humor and facial expressions, and she rolls her eyes and puts a hand on her hip. Reverend Terri looked forward to opening the church doors but would wait until it was safest to do so. "When we can gather together again," she said, "I think the place will be packed."

People missed the social aspect of going to church, but Joy MCC planned to continue its digital initiatives postpandemic. They've helped grow the number of folks who can attend. Viewers have watched services from Miami to Brazil to Malta. I was one of these virtual attendees who found a church community while quarantined. Joy MCC stood less than ten miles away from some of Orlando's theme parks like The Holy Land Experience. Those attractions gave visitors pyrotechnic performances and larger-than-life experiences. People could escape their daily lives there, while Joy MCC—and places like it—let people come home. They gave Floridians a second chance to be who they already knew they were.

Acknowledgments

Thank you to the many Floridians who trusted me with their stories, insights, laughter, and tears. This book contains only a portion of the interviews I conducted for this book, but every person I talked to helped shape the project.

To early section readers: Dahlia El-Shafei, Anna Elias, Janet Keeler, Ciera Horton McElroy, Bernardo Motta, Rev Miranda, Allison Pinkerton, Florentina Staigers, and Debbie Weaver.

I owe Florida favors to Carlynn Crosby and Jessica "Snake Woman" Smith.

To my agent, Lauren MacLeod, who braved snake chapters even though she doesn't "trust animals with poison teeth and no arms or legs."

To my editor, Sian Hunter, for her thoughtful feedback, thoroughness, and guidance—also, for reining in my Nancy Grace references. I'd like to thank the entire staff of University Press of Florida for their hard work as well as the UPF peer reviewers: R1, Cathy Salustri, Jim Ross, and Julie Marie Wade.

To the editors of the following publications in which parts of my reporting previously appeared:

Salon: "The Florida Woman Trying to Break Free of Being 'Florida Woman'"

The Guardian: "Hiiiiissssss! Why Florida Needs Your Help to Hunt Pythons Down"

The Nation: "How Students Made an Off-Campus Protest a Movement"

VICE: "Disney May Rule, but Gator Wrestling and Roadside Attractions Remain in Florida"

I included lines of poetry from my collection *Florida Man: Poems* (Red Flag Poetry, 2018).

I'm grateful for the support of the University of South Florida–St. Petersburg and the *Salon* Young Americans reporting fellowship.

All my love to Mom, Gramel, John, and my other family members who help make the Sunshine State magical for me.

Notes

Because Florida

"The state is just everything": "John Mulaney Explains Why Comedians Always Make Fun of Florida," *Late Night with Seth Meyers*, May 1, 2018, YouTube video, 5:12, https://www.youtube.com/watch?v=bdNgEbLij5M.

assaulted for a Facebook friend request snub: Cox Group National Desk Content, "Florida Woman Assaults Grandmother for Facebook Friend Snub, Police Say," *Atlanta Journal-Constitution*, December 18, 2014, https://www.ajc.com/news/national/florida-woman-assaults-grandmother-for-facebook-friend-snub-police-say/3WC8XPr7crjpWbvABEWCUL/.

"Fights to Keep Her Pet Alligator": Avianne Tan, "Florida Woman Fights to Keep Her Pet Alligator Who Wears Clothes and 'Rides' ATVs," ABC News, March 17, 2016, https://abcnews.go.com/US/florida-woman-fights-pet-alligator-wears-clothesrides/story?id=37717980.

"Snake Farm Shooting": Kyle Munzenrieder, "Snake Farm Shooting: Tom Crutchfield and Business Partner Bruce Stephenson Involved in Deadly Argument," *Miami New Times*, April 1, 2011, https://www.miaminewtimes.com/news/snake-farm-shooting-tom-crutchfield-and-business-partner-bruce-stephenson-involved-in-deadly-argument-6556579.

Deborah Clark had worked: Deborah Clark, interview by the author, September 2016.

The voting system had been solid: Ibid.

Florida and other states: Ibid.

"Land of Recounts and Contested Elections": Patricia Mazzei and Frances Robles, "It's Déjà Vu in Florida, Land of Recounts and Contested Elections," *New York Times*, November 9, 2018, https://www.nytimes.com/2018/11/09/us/florida-ballots-recount-scott-nelson-gillum-desantis.html.

the search term first spiked: https://trends.google.com/trends/explore?date=all&geo=US&q=%22Florida%20Man%22.

"Where Do You Live": *Florida Agriculturist* (DeLand), July 31, 1878, https://ufdc.ufl.edu/UF00047911/00624/4x.

300 bushels of sweet potatoes: Ibid.

stick an orange seed in the ground: Ibid.

"exaggerated stories": Ibid.

More than 21 million people: "QuickFacts: Florida," United States Census Bureau (2018), https://www.census.gov/quickfacts/FL.

"without any real guarantee that baseball": Philip Belcastro, "Poverty, Planning, Policy and Race: Urban Design in St. Petersburg, Florida, since 1965" (honors thesis, University of South Florida–St. Petersburg, 2017).

"emptied their weapons": Samuel Johnson, "Historical Amnesia about Lynching in St. Petersburg: The John Evans Plaque," WMNF, May 16, 2015, https://www.wmnf.org/historical-amnesia-the-john-evans-plaque/.

FLORIDA MAN THEORY

Parts of the writing and reporting of this story originally appeared in my article "'The Florida Woman Trying to Break Free of Being 'Florida Woman,'" published on Salon.com, August 27, 2017, https://www.salon.com/control/2017/08/27/the-florida-woman-trying-to-break-free-of-being-florida-woman/?fb_comment_id= 1390755524371838_1390868804360510.

"Florida Man in Pirate Costume": Dole Murphy, "Florida Man in Pirate Costume Arrested for Firing Black-Powder Guns," *New York Daily News*, July 6, 2015, https://www.nydailynews.com/news/national/ florida-man-pirate-costume-busted-black-powder-blasts-article-1.2283247.

"Florida Man Learns": Justin Kirkland, "The 90 Wildest Florida Man Headlines of 2019 (So Far)," *Esquire*, April 1, 2019, https://www.esquire.com/ news-politics/a26899191/florida-man-headlines-2019/.

"Florida Woman Charged with Stealing": Ashley Harding and Corley Peel, "Florida Woman Charged with Stealing Rental Car Says 'Demons Took It,'" News4Jax, March 8, 2019, https://www.news4jax.com/news/2019/03/08/ florida-woman-charged-with-stealing-rental-car-says-demons-took-it/.

In the mid-2000s, Fark.com: "Florida Man," KnowYourMeme, April 5, 2018, http://knowyourmeme.com/memes/florida-man.

A guy had reportedly smoked bath salts: This story took on a mythology of its own. In 2016, *Miami New Times* ran the headline, "Bath Salts Didn't Cause the Miami Cannibal Attack, Scientists Say." The publication's Tim Elfrink wrote, "[A] police spokesman speculated that the synthetic drug might have driven Eugene's madness. The only problem is that bath salts were never found in Eugene's body in any postmortem exams" (https://www.miaminewtimes.com/news/ bath-salts-didnt-cause-the-miami-cannibal-attack-scientists-say-6547371).

The victim went through a slow: WSVN, "Miami Cannibal Attack Victim Recovering," CNN, May 22, 2013, https://www.cnn.com/videos/ us/2013/05/22/wsvn-pkg-cannibal-attack-update.wsvn.

"Yankee nightmare in human form": John Lingan, "America's Long, Rich History of Trashing Poor Whites," *Pacific Standard*, June 14, 2017, https:// psmag.com/news/americas-long-rich-history-of-trashing-poor-whites.

An associate editor at *GQ*: Logan Hill, "Is It Okay to Laugh at Florida Man?," *Washington Post*, July 15, 2019, https://www.washingtonpost.com/news/ magazine/wp/2019/07/15/feature/is-it-okay-to-laugh-at-florida-man-2/.

The account received nearly 64,000 followers: "Florida Man," KnowYourMeme, April 5, 2018, http://knowyourmeme.com/memes/florida-man.

"attack his roommate with a sword": Kelsey Wheatcroft, "EPD: Evansville Man Tries to Attack Roommate with Sword," 14 News, January 19, 2011, https://www.14news.com/story/13871802/epd-evansville-man-attacks-roommate-with-sword/.

"news about the terrible superhero": r/FloridaMan, https://www.reddit.com/r/FloridaMan/. I last checked the r/FloridaMan member count on August 8, 2020, and it counted 684,701 members.

an attempt to trademark "Florida Man": Craig Pittman, "Florida Man vs. Florida Man: He Wants to Trademark 'Florida Man' before Someone Else Does," *Tampa Bay Times*, May 15, 2019, https://www.tampabay.com/environment/florida-man-vs-florida-man-he-wants-to-trademark-florida-man-before-someone-else-does-20190514/.

"inner Florida Man": David Britton, "Which 'Florida Man' Are You?," *Daily Dot*, March 21, 2019, https://www.dailydot.com/unclick/florida-man-birthday-twitter-meme/.

"rogue's paradise": Christopher Waldrep, "'A Rogue's Paradise': Crime and Punishment in Antebellum Florida, 1821–1861," *Journal of the Early Republic* 2 (1998): 343.

"Cutting Affray": *Banner* (Live Oak, FL), September 27, 1895, https://ufdc.ufl.edu/UF00055758/00001/2.

Sam's brother ran: Ibid.

"blood was seen": Ibid.

"stroll by sunlight": "Killed His Sweetheart," *Alachua Advocate* (Gainesville, FL), May 30, 1883, http://ufdc.ufl.edu/UF00054870/00001/2.

"held an inquest": Ibid.

"Edna May's recipe": Edna May, "Chorus Girls Best of Wives for Rich Men," *Alachua Booster* (Gainesville, FL), February 2, 1912, https://ufdc.ufl.edu/AA00020203/00001/1x.

Only about a half million folks: "Florida. Resident Population and Apportionment of the U.S. House of Representatives," United States Census Bureau (2000), https://www.census.gov/dmd/www/resapport/states/florida.pdf.

"health & pleasure seekers paradise": Advertisement of the Plant System including the Tampa Bay Hotel—Tampa, Florida, 1896, black-and-white photoprint, 10 × 8 in., Florida Memory, State Archives of Florida, https://www.floridamemory.com/items/show/33374.

days as both invigorating: "Volusia and Brevard Counties," *Florida Agriculturist* (DeLand, FL), July 19, 1882, https://ufdc.ufl.edu/UF00047911/00543/3x.

Florida's population balloon: "Florida. Resident Population and Apportionment," United States Census Bureau, https://www.census.gov/dmd/www/resapport/states/florida.pdf.

"Wave of Palm Tree Thefts": Justin Blum, "Homeowners Report Wave of Palm Tree Thefts," *St. Petersburg Times*, April 12, 1995, https://news.google.com/

newspapers?nid=feST4K8JoscC &dat=19950412&printsec=frontpage&hl =en.

"Florida Man" because of journalism basics: Janet Keeler, interview by the author, May 2018.

"Florida was the first state": Craig Pittman qtd. in "Who Is 'Florida Man'? Desi Lydic Investigates," *The Daily Show with Trevor Noah*, YouTube video, 7:12, November 2, 2018, https://www.youtube.com/watch?v=UD9LEPML8uk.

"That Florida Man": Catherine Cameron, email to the author, June 2, 2016.

"It is quite the stigma": Catherine Cameron, interview by the author, June 2, 2016.

helped Florida become the state: Joseph Eagleton "Walking on Sunshine Laws: How Florida's Free Press History in the U.S. Supreme Court Undermines Open Government," *Florida Bar Journal*, September/October 2012, https://www.floridabar.org/the-florida-bar-journal/walking-on-sunshine-laws-how-floridas-free-press-history-in-the-u-s-supreme-court-undermines-open-government/.

public records exemptions created a lag: Catherine Cameron interview.

One of these sites allegedly took: Samantha Schmidt, "This Site Will Remove Your Mug Shot—for a Price, Authorities Say: Its Owners Are Charged with Extortion," *Washington Post*, "Morning Mix," May 18, 2018, https://www.washingtonpost.com/news/morning-mix/wp/2018/05/18/this-site-will-remove-your-mug-shot-for-a-price-now-its-owners-are-charged-with-extortion/?utm_ term=.1173f481098b.

"Florida Woman Repeatedly Slapped Her Grandmother": TheSource.com, "Florida Woman Repeatedly Slapped Her Grandmother for Rejecting Her Friend Request on Facebook," December 14, 2014, https://thesource.com/2014/12/19/a-florida-woman-repeatedly-slapped-her-grandmother-for-rejecting-her-friend-request-on-facebook/.

"You could have left out any references": Commenter UncleCCClaudius on the article "Florida Woman Assaults Grandmother for Denying Facebook Request," Jezebel.com, December 21, 2014, https://jezebel.com/florida-woman-assaults-grandmother-for-denying-facebook-1673926448.

"True; Pinellas County": Rebecca Rose, "Florida Woman Assaults Grandmother for Denying Facebook Request," Jezebel.com, December 21, 2014, https://jezebel.com/florida-woman-assaults-grandmother-for-denying-facebook-1673926448.

"It bothered me that Nancy Grace": Rachel Hayes, interview by the author, December 2015.

dinner was going fine: Rebecca Hayes, interview by the author, January 2016.

"about six foot, one inch and very German": Rachel Hayes interview.

"This evening def was at vic's residence": Case No. 14–20281-CF State of Florida VS. Hayes, Rachel, Complaint/Arrest Affidavit, County Court, Pinellas County, FL., Docket #1619235.

the argument was a family dispute: Rebecca Hayes interview.

Rachel boarded a Greyhound bus: Rachel Hayes interview.

"an inspiration to us all": Interviewee names withheld for anonymity.

"I can finally have a normal bank account": Rachel Hayes interview.
"If you would have told me": Rachel Hayes, Facebook, April 3, 2016, https://
www.facebook.com/moonpie.hayes/posts/1180655568620436.

OF THE STORM

They needed to include a drawing: City of Largo, Permits, retrieved May 16,
2019, from https://www.largo.com/connect/living_in_largo/permits_and_
planning/building_permits/permits.php.
area hadn't experienced: Phil McCausland, "Some in Tampa Bay Unsure
What to Expect from Hurricane Irma," NBC News, September
10, 2017, https://www.nbcnews.com/storyline/ hurricane-irma/
some-tampa-bay-unsure-what-expect-hurricane-irma-n800171.
"a vicious storm": Christopher Geist, "The Hurricane in History,"
Colonial Williamsburg Journal (Winter 2005), https://research.
colonialwilliamsburg.org/library/materials/periodicals/indexes/view/index.
cfm?type=journal&id=1468.
Some hurricanes started: Jennifer Collins, interview by the author, June 2019.
These mad, furious winds: Sarah Cervone, "Eye on the Storm," in *Disasters in
Paradise: Natural Hazards, Social Vulnerability, and Development Decisions*,
ed. Amanda D. Concha-Holmes, Anthony Oliver-Smith et al. (Lanham, MD:
Lexington, 2019), 27.
"long lists of dead": "Property Loss Many Millions, Hundreds Hurt," *St.
Petersburg Times*, September 19, 1928, https://news.google.com/newspapers?
nid=feST4K8JoscC&dat=19280919&printsec=frontpage&hl=en.
around 2,500 Floridians died: Nicole Sterghos Brochu, "Florida's Forgotten
Storm: The Hurricane of 1928," *Sun-Sentinel* (pdf), September 14, 2003,
http://liberalstudiesguides.ca/wp-content/uploads/sites/2/2017/04/
Floridas-forgotten-storm_-The-Hurricane-of-1928-Sun-Sentinel.pdf.
Morgan acted like a weather reporter: Morgan Guigon, interview by the
author, June 2019.
Irma destroyed: John P. Cangialosi, Andrew S. Latto, and Robbie Berg,
"National Hurricane Center Tropical Cyclone Report: Hurricane Irma,"
National Hurricane Center, June 30, 2018, https://www.nhc.noaa.gov/data/
tcr/AL112017_Irma.pdf.
About one thousand homes sustained: Ibid.
Nearly 6.8 million Floridians left: "Hurricane Irma Evacuation," Florida
Association of Counties, http://factor.fl-counties.com/hurricane-irma-
evacuation .
she wanted to figure out why: Jennifer Collins, interview by the author, June
2019.

A CONFEDERACY OF REENACTORS

A Florida convention voted: *Journal of the Proceedings of the Convention of the
People of Florida*, 31–32, https://archive.org/details/journalofproceedooflor/
page/30, 31.
Florida's population totaled: According to the 1860 census, Florida's

population breakdown: 77,747 "white"; 932 "free colored"; and 61,754 "slave" (https://www2.census.gov/library/publications/decennial/1860/population/1860a-09.pdf).

Most of those enslaved people: Larry Rivers, *Slavery in Florida: Territorial Days to Emancipation* (Gainesville: University Press of Florida, 2000), 18–19.

"rapid spread of Northern fanaticism": *Journal of the Proceedings of the Convention of the People of Florida*, 3.

"forgotten state of the Civil War": "Florida in the Civil War," State Archives of Florida, https://www.floridamemory.com/onlineclassroom/floridacivilwar/.

a war that saw upward of 850,000 deaths: For nearly a century, the Civil War death toll had been widely accepted as nearly 620,000, but in 2011 J. David Hacker used "demographic methods and sophisticated statistical software" to argue for an increased total. He documents his findings and calculations in "A Census-Based Count of the Civil War Dead: With Introductory Remarks by James M. McPherson," *Civil War History* 57, no. 4 (2011): 307–48, https://www.pdcnet.org/cwh/content/cwh_2011_0057_0004_0307_0348.

Nearly 1,500 all-volunteer reenactors: "Welcome to the Brooksville Raid," Hernando Historical Museum, http://hernandohistoricalmuseumassoc.com/raid/index.htm.

"made by an old man in Virginia": Travis Stevens, interview by the author, January 2019.

laid out according to U.S. Army Regs–1861: Keith Kohl, interview by the author, January 2019.

grandchildren began to give talks at schools: Rory Turner, "Bloodless Battles: The Civil War Reenacted," *TDR* (1988–) 34, no. 4 (1990): 123–36.

Around 40 million Americans: Michael Morrison and Robert May, "The Limitations of Classroom Media: Ken Burns' Civil War Series as a Test Case," *Journal of American Culture* 19, no. 3 (1996): 39–49.

Those productions drew criticism: Robert Brent Toplin, ed., *Ken Burns's The Civil War: Historians Respond* (New York: Oxford University Press, 1996).

Keith had moved: Keith Kohl interview.

Other weaponry guidelines: from the Brooksville Raid Reenactment "Safety Guidelines" (revised 10/21/2016), http://brooksvilleraidreenactment.com/reenactor-forms/.

"glorified treason and a hateful history": "When Heritage Means Hate," NAACP, https://www.naacp.org/field-resources/confederate-symbols/.

In 2015, a couple thousand people: CBS News, "Confederate Flag Rally Draws Thousands, Sparks Gunfire in Florida," July 13, 2015, https://www.cbsnews.com/news/confederate-flag-rally-draws-thousands-sparks-gunfire-in-florida/.

The second-largest Confederate flag: Roadside America, "World's 2nd Largest Confederate Flag," RoadsideAmerica.com, https://www.roadsideamerica.com/story/19407.

"If you're a Union reenactor": Chuck Munson, interview by the author, January 2019.

A man dressed as: Ray Sanchez, Kaylee Hartung, and Devon M. Sayers, "Man in Confederate Uniform Confronted by Charlottesville Residents," CNN, August 15, 2017, https://www.cnn.com/2017/08/15/us/charlottesville-lee-park-confrontation/index.html.

"At this point": Trae Crowder qtd. in Cathy Salustri's "Liberal Redneck Trae Crowder Will Make You Laugh Your Southern Heart out Friday Night at the Straz Center in Tampa," *Creative Loafing,* February 27, 2009, https://www.cltampa.com/artsentertainment/comedy/article/ 21049025/liberal-redneck-trae-crowder-friday-night-at-the-straz-center-in-tampa.

The FBI found an explosive: Dennette Rybiski (FBI Richmond), "Public's Assistance Requested after Incident Occurring at Cedar Creek and Belle Grove National Historical Park," October 15, 2017, https://www.fbi.gov/contact-us/field-offices/richmond/news/press-releases/publics-assistance-requested-after-incident-occurring-at-cedar-creek-and-belle-grove-national-historical-park.

the divisive political climate worried everybody: Jacob McLaughlin, interview by the author, January 2019.

"Back then, they believed": Jeff Hardy, interview by the author, January 2019.

"even if most individuals in Florida": Tracy J. Revels, *Grander in Her Daughters: Florida's Women during the Civil War* (Columbia: University of South Carolina Press, 2004), 3.

Normally, the reenactors performed: Keith Kohl interview.

More than 15,000 Floridians: Seth Weitz, "From Territory to Twenty-Seventh State," in *A Forgotten Front: Florida during the Civil War Era,* edited by Jonathan C. Sheppard and Seth Weitz (Tuscaloosa: University of Alabama Press, 2018).

a few women who could shoot: Jeff Hardy interview.

"cut a swath of destruction": Jennifer Hawley, "Florida's Civil War Soldiers" (master's thesis, University of South Florida, 2005, 43, https://scholarcommons.usf.edu/etd/2922/).

"interdict the flow of cattle": Robert A Taylor, "Rebel Beef: Florida Cattle and the Confederate Army, 1862–1864," *Florida Historical Quarterly* 67, no. 1 (1988): 15–31, http://www.jstor.org/stable/30147921.

"a failure; in other words": "Letters from Men of the 40th Massachusetts Mounted Infantry," https://battleofolustee.org/letters/40th-mass2.htm.

McLeod moved to Florida: "McLeod Diary," State Archives of Florida, https://www.floridamemory.com/items/show/260495.

"3 of our men were wounded": Ibid.

"negroes 700 & whites 300": Ibid.

"lying in the ditches": Ibid.

They discussed why: Chuck Munson interview.

"in social change and feels": Jacob McLaughlin, interview by the author, January 2019.

white beards and round bellies: Mark Guarino, "Will Civil War Re-enactments Die Out?," *Washington Post,* August 25, 2017, https://www.washingtonpost.com/entertainment/museums/will-civil-war-reenactments-die-out/2017/08/25/f43c6bc0–874b-11e7-a50f-e0d4e6ec070a_story.html.

An estimated 10 to 20 percent: Jim Murphy, *The Boys' War: Confederate and Union Soldiers Talk about the Civil War* (New York: Clarion, 1990).

three-million-plus soldiers: Exact Civil War numbers—of soldiers, death toll—cannot be calculated due to incomplete records. Thomas Leonard Livermore gets into the details in *Numbers and Losses in the Civil War in America, 1861–65.* New York: Houghton, Mifflin, 1900.

civilians had tried to continue: Genie Stracuzzi, interview by the author, January 2019.

"My whole unit was destroyed": Blake Cooper, interview by the author, January 2019.

"would be horrified to see teenagers": Jacob McLaughlin, correspondence with the author, November 2019.

"The soldiers raided": Genie Stracuzzi interview.

H. K. didn't reenact: H. K. Edgerton, interview by the author, January 2019.

free African Americans: John Coski, "Myth: Thousands of Enslaved and Free African American Soldiers Fought for the Confederacy," The American Civil War Museum, https://acwm.org/blog/myths-misunderstandings-black-confederates.

"race traitors": John Stauffer, "Yes, There Were Black Confederates: Here's Why," *The Root*, January 20, 2015, https://www.theroot.com/yes-there-were-black-confederates-here-s-why-1790858546.

black men who fought: H. K. Edgerton interview.

the good fight: Mark Norman, "God bless you sir. Keep up the good fight!," Facebook, December 27, 2019.

Uncle Tom: Btx3, "Black Confederate' Fool Meets Real Confederate KKK," *Btx3's Blog*, May 10, 2016, https://btx3.wordpress.com/2016/05/10/black-confederate-fool-meets-real-confederate-kkk/.

"Have you collected": Tiffany Davis, interview, January 2019.

LANDSCAPE WITH CRACKERS

Nine of the nation's: "Florida Agriculture: Fast Facts 2018," University of Florida's Institute of Food and Agricultural Sciences, 2018, https://ifas.ufl.edu/media/ifasufledu/ifas-dark-blue/docs/pdf/impact/ICS_FloridaAgFactsBooklet2018.web.pdf.

15 percent of the state's land: Alan Hodges, Christa D. Court, Mohammad Rahmani, and Caleb A. Stair, "Economic Contributions of Beef and Dairy Cattle and Allied Industries in Florida in 2017," University of Florida Institute of Food and Agricultural Sciences (2017), https://fred.ifas. ufl.edu/DEStudio/PDF/2017CattleIndustry/Full%20Report%20%20Economic%20Contributions%20of%20Cattle%202017.pdf.

"We've got eight generations": Cary Lightsey, interview by the author, July 2019.

Spaniards brought the invasive hogs: William M. Giuliano, "Wild Hogs in Florida: Ecology and Management," IFAS WEC277, University of Florida Institute of Food and Agricultural Sciences, Gainesville (2010).

Anywhere from 500,000 to a million: Florida Department of Agriculture and

Consumer Services, Division of Animal Industry, State Veterinarian's Office, August 2018, https://www.fdacs.gov/content/download/71109/file/Feral-Swine-Brochure-English.pdf.

Male hogs averaged: Ibid.

if nutrition was poor, they ate: Giuliano, "Wild Hogs in Florida."

"roving hogs": "Those Hogs Again," *Florida Agriculturist* (DeLand), January 31, 1883, https://ufdc.ufl.edu/UF00047911/00405/1x.

Feral hogs hunted: Nathan W. Seward, Kurt C. VerCauteren, Gary W. Witmer, and Richard M. Engeman, "Feral Swine Impacts on Agriculture and the Environment," *Sheep & Goat Research Journal* (2004): 12.

"I don't hunt": Cary Lightsey interview.

met in high school: Marcia Lightsey, interview by the author, September 2019.

woke up in a hospital room: Cary Lightsey interview.

hides of those restaurant cows: John A Marchello and Elaine V. Marchello, "Contributions to Society: Slaughter By-products," *Encyclopedia of Animal Science* (New York: Marcel Dekker, 2004), 258–60.

promote the cattle industry: "About Us," Florida Cattlewomen, https://www.floridacattlemen.org/fcw/.

fourteen to eighteen years: Cary Lightsey interview.

dates to the Spanish conquistadors: Lewis L. Yarlett, "History of the Florida Cattle Industry," *Rangelands Archives* 7, no. 5 (1985): 205–7.

around 1,620 head of cattle: Ibid.

1.68 million head: "Southern Region News Release Cattle Inventory," United States Department of Agriculture National Agricultural Statistics Service, January 31, 2020, https://www.nass.usda.gov/Statistics_by_State/Regional_Office/Southern/includes/Publications/Livestock_Releases/Cattle_Inventory/Cattle2020a.pdf.

Cattle proved Florida's major contribution: Yarlett, "History of the Florida Cattle Industry," 205–7.

family's stock went to the Confederacy: Cary Lightsey interview.

"cowmen" or "cow hunters": Robert Stone, *Florida Cattle Ranching: Five Centuries of Tradition* (Kissimmee: Florida Cattlemen's Foundation, 2013), 8.

cowman and Cracker: Ibid.

"the white slave driver": Urban Dictionary.com, s.v. "Cracker," https://www.urbandictionary.com/define.php?term=Cracker.

"has almost always been used disparagingly": Grady McWhiney, *Cracker Culture: Celtic Ways in the Old South* (Tuscaloosa: University of Alabama Press, 1989), xiii–xix.

In 1712, his ancestors: Cary Lightsey interview.

"three or five or ten cents an acre": Cary Lightsey interview. Early pioneer acreage was documented by Charles Barnard and John Jones in *Farm Real Estate Values in the United States by Counties, 1850–1982*, No. 1487–2016–122545, 1987. The earliest official record for Polk County begins in 1880 and lists the "average value of farmland per acre" of the area at one dollar.

nearly $1.3 million: Tanner Latham, "A Legacy of Land," *FarmLife*, https://myfarmlife.com/2010/legacy-of-land/.

wondered if they should go: Marcia Lightsey interview.

sometimes ate the wild hogs: Latham, "A Legacy of Land."

sell them to a hunting reserve: Cary Lightsey interview.

the site listed: "Florida Farms for Sale," Farmflip.com. These prices were the highest and lowest listed on September 29, 2019, https://www.farmflip.com/farms-for-sale/florida/hp-s.

"nutritional deficiencies and tick fever": Yarlett, "History of the Florida Cattle Industry," 205–7.

In the late 1890s, cattle: "Cattle in Florida," *Tropical Sun* (Juno Beach, FL), April 7, 1892, https://ufdc.ufl.edu/UF00075915/00478/2x.

"The beef steers sleek": "An Agricultural Ode," *Florida Agriculturist* (DeLand), January 1, 1910, https://ufdc.ufl.edu/UF00047911/01085/27x.

vast quantity of unproductive: "Stock Raising in Florida," *Florida Agriculturist* (DeLand), January 17, 1883, https://ufdc.ufl.edu/UF00047911/00403/4x.

proper fencing: Ibid.

"improved pasture era": Yarlett, "History of the Florida Cattle Industry," 205–7.

nutrients occurred in nature: Kristen Miller, "State Laws Banning Phosphorus Fertilizer Use" (2012): 1–4, Connecticut General Assembly, Office of Legislative Research, Hartford, https://www.cga.ct.gov/2012/rpt/2012-R-0076.htm.

At one point, a reported: Sarah Hollenbeck, "33.48 Tons of Dead Fish Collected in Pinellas County as Red Tide Bloom Lingers," *ABC Action News*, September 12, 2018, https://www.abcactionnews.com/news/region-pinellas/3348-tons-of-dead-fish-collected-in-pinellas-county-as-red-tide-bloom-lingers.

central Florida ranches affected: John Fauth, interview by the author, September 2018.

improved pastures often harbored: Patrick Bohlen, interview by the author, September 2018.

"Having clean land": Cary Lightsey interview.

The family placed over 90 percent: Ibid.

These were agreements: "Conservation Easements," University of Florida's Institute of Food and Agricultural Sciences, http://www.sfrc.ufl.edu/Extension/florida_forestry_ information/planningandassistance/conservation_easements.html.

The then Warner student: Mikayla Allison, interview by the author, September 2019.

The cowboys-for-hire: Cary Lightsey interview.

corn, a staple ingredient: "Summary of Florida Corn Production," University of Florida's Institute of Food and Agricultural Sciences (Florida Corn Insect Identification Guide), https://erec.ifas.ufl.edu/fciig/sfcp.htm.

"Oh, have I got": Doyle Carlton III, interview by the author, July 2019.

He'd found Jesus: Ibid.

"animal cruelty investigative organization": Animal Recovery Mission (ARM), https://animalrecoverymission.org/about-arm/.

national headlines: Travis Andrews, "Undercover Video Shows Farmworkers

Beating Cows with Metal Rods: Police Are Investigating the Dairy,"
Washington Post, November 13, 2017, https://www.washingtonpost.com/
news/morning-mix/wp/2017/11/13/undercover-video-shows-farmworkers-
beating-cows-with-metal-rods/?noredirect=on#comments.

Activists protested: Mike Opperman, "Florida Producer Survives Undercover
Video Attack," *Farm Journal's MILK*, May 6, 2019, https://www.milkbusiness.
com/article/florida-producer-survives-undercover-video-attack.

three attempted to flee the country: Monique Madan, "They Were Caught
Beating up and Kicking Cows, But Then Fled the Country, Cops Say," *Miami
Herald*, November 27, 2017, https://www.miamiherald.com/news/state/
florida/article186799788.html.

In the past, environmentalists: Doyle Carlton III interview.

huge corporations have been known: Codi Gauker, "The Impacts of
Sustainable and Industrial Agriculture on Human Health," Moravian
College, 2010, https://www.sustainlv.org/one/wp-content/uploads/Food-
Impacts-on-Health.pdf.

[ICE] arrested 680 undocumented workers: Richard Gonzales, "Mississippi
Immigration Raids Lead to Arrests of Hundreds of Workers," NPR,
August 7, 2019, https://www.npr.org/2019/08/07/749243985/
mississippi-immigration-raids-net-hundreds-of-workers.

YOUNG AND BEAUTIFUL FOREVER

"Mom said I'd been": Randy Phoenix, interview by the author, July 2019.

She was also a founding board member: "Nadine Smith," Equality Florida,
2018, https://www.eqfl.org/nadine-smith.

More than twenty-five years of activism: Nadine Smith, interview by the
author, May 2018.

"My wife was black": George Smith, interview by the author, May 2018.

She saw two paths: Nadine Smith interview.

The Human Rights Task Force of Florida: Ibid.

"one of the visionaries": Stratton Pollitzer, interview by the author, May 2018.

Florida played an important role: Ibid.

"If she was a white guy": Elizabeth Schwartz interview, May 2018.

Brandon and others around him: Brandon Wolf qtd. in Lilli Petersen's "Pulse
Shooting Survivor Brandon Wolf Explains Why He Speaks out for Gun
Policy Reform," Elite Daily, June 12, 2019, https://www.elitedaily.com/p/
pulse-shooting-survivor-brandon-wolf-explains-why-he-speaks-out-for-gun-
policy-reform-17996133.

He'd never felt such heartbreak: Brandon Wolf, interview by the author, June
2020.

comprehensive GSA guides: "About," The Dru Project, http://thedruproject.
org/about.

Brandon hadn't been much involved: Brandon Wolf interview.

nearly 120,000 people donated: Equality Florida, "Support Victims of Pulse
Shooting," GoFundMe, created June 12, 2016, https://www.gofundme.com/
PulseVictimsFund.

These funds were designated for victims: Nadine Smith interview.

Nadine and Equality Florida have approached: Shannon Minter, interview by the author, May 2018.

They had a falling out: Nadine Smith interview.

If a church member: George Smith interview.

Equality Florida planned: Nadine Smith interview.

The organization wanted: "Issues Overview," Equality Florida, https://www.eqfl.org/Issues_Overview.

"It started becoming clear": Walter Latimer, interview by the author, June 2019.

Publications didn't reach out: Ibid.

"LGBT seniors have been forgotten": Steve McCloud, interview by the author, June 2019.

Vitambi's name derived: Martin Ruddock, interview by the author, June 2019.

Some of these men: Ibid.

grown up in Nashville, Tennessee: Steve McCloud interview.

This was typical: Martin Ruddock interview.

He had run the conservation corps: Steve McCloud interview.

listed nearly fifty stateside: "Florida Gay Campgrounds," GayCampingUSA.com., http://www.gaycampingusa.com/florida.html.

Wilton Manors was the first: Jacob Ogles, "Wilton Manors Elects All Openly Gay City Commission," Florida Politics, November 7, 2018, https://floridapolitics.com/archives/280617-wilton-manors-elects-all-openly-gay-city-commission.

"second gayest city in America": "LGBT+ Life in Wilton Manors," City of Wilton Manors, https://www.wiltonmanors.com/ 290/ LGBT-Life-in-Wilton-Manors.

he'd known people: Martin Ruddock interview.

Manny and Francisco: The couple didn't want me to publish their last name for privacy reasons.

seventy-four-year-old Francisco immigrated: Francisco, interview by the author, June 2019.

"We don't feel we are less privileged": Manny, interview by the author, June 2019.

seen a shift: Francisco interview.

one reason LGBTQ seniors: Steve McCloud interview.

The friend had taken a caregiver's class: Ibid.

BRIEF ENCOUNTERS WITH ALLIGATORS

They weren't actual lizards: Peter Dodson, "Allure of El Lagarto—Why Do Dinosaur Paleontologists Love Alligators, Crocodiles, and Their Kin?," The Anatomical Record Part A: Discoveries in Molecular, Cellular, and Evolutionary Biology 274, no. 2 (2003): 887–90.

"found these monsters so numerous": "Floridiana," Florida Agriculturist (DeLand), February 26, 1879, 5, https://ufdc.ufl.edu/UF00047911/00653/5x.

"interrupted by alligators": "Floridiana," *Florida Agriculturist* (DeLand), March 5, 1879, 5, https://ufdc.ufl.edu/UF00047911/00654/5x.

"gators lashed the water": Ibid.

"huge alligators": Reprint of a promotional news piece on DeLeon Springs in Volusia County, 1889, State Archives of Florida, https://www.floridamemory.com/items/show/297294.

"placed a rifle ball": Ibid.

"muck, shells, alligators": "Alligators as Fertilizer," *Florida Agriculturist* (DeLand), July 31, 1878, 4, https://ufdc.ufl.edu/UF00047911/00624/4x.

"for the prejudice against": "Floridiana," *Florida Agriculturist*, February 26, 1879, 4, https://ufdc.ufl.edu/UF00047911/00653/4x.

the big lizards climbed: Tim Williams, interview by the author, February 2017.

The most popular roadsides: Margot Ammidown, "Edens, Underworlds, and Shrines: Florida's Small Tourist Attractions," *Journal of Decorative and Propaganda Arts* 23 (1998): 239–59, doi:10.2307/1504171.

In 1967, the American alligator: This endangered classification preceded the Endangered Species Act of 1973. "American Alligator: *Alligator mississippiensis*," U.S. Fish & Wildlife Services, February 2008, https://www.fws.gov/uploadedFiles/American-Alligator-Fact-Sheet.pdf.

It's currently illegal: Florida Statute 379.409, "Illegal killing, possessing, or capturing of alligators or other crocodilia or eggs; confiscation of equipment," 2019, http://www.leg.state.fl.us/statutes/index.cfm?App_mode=Display_Statute&URL=0300-0399/0379/Sections/0379.409.html.

In 2019, an estimated 1.3 million gators: This population was estimated by the Florida Fish and Wildlife Commission: https://myfwc.com/wildlifehabitats/wildlife/alligator/snap/.

among Florida's 21 million: "QuickFacts: Florida (2018)," United States Census Bureau, https://www.census.gov/quickfacts/FL.

About a third of a gator's nest: "Alligator Facts," Florida Fish and Wildlife Conservation Commission, https://myfwc.com/wildlifehabitats/wildlife/alligator/facts/.

His father, George: Clint Bridges, interview by the author, February 2017.

"Alligator wrestling itself": Dialogue from Paul Bedard's show at Everglades Holiday Park in February 2017.

A group of cadets: Parts of the writing and reporting of this story originally appeared in a different form in my article "Gator Wrestling Is Preserving Florida's Independent Tourism Industry," published in *VICE*, August 17, 2017, https://www.vice.com/en_us/article/vvkznb/disney-may-rule-but-gator-wrestling-and-roadside-attractions-remain-in-florida-v24n3.

vacationed from Arizona: Dean Cross, interview by the author, February 2017.

He moved to the Florida Keys: "Everglades Holiday Park Showcase: Paul Bedard of the Gator Boys," *Everglades Holiday Park* (blog), December 8, 2014, https://www.evergladesholidaypark.com/paul-bedard-gator-boys/.

They can grow more than: Steven G. Platt, Ruth M. Elsey, Thomas R. Rainwater, and Mike Fredenberg, "A Critical Analysis of a Historic Size

NOTES TO PAGES 82–85 · 161

Record for the American Alligator," *Southeastern Naturalist* 17, no. 4 (November 1, 2018).

weigh more than 1,000 pounds: Florida Fish and Wildlife Conservation Commission, "Alligator Facts: Size," https://myfwc.com/wildlifehabitats/wildlife/alligator/facts/.

"Florida Man Arrested for Allegedly": Megan McCluskey, "Florida Man Arrested for Allegedly Throwing Live Alligator into Wendy's Drive-Thru Window," *Time*, February 9, 2016, https://time.com/4214021/florida-man-throws-alligator-into-wendys-drive-thru-window/.

primarily compensated: "How to Be a Nuisance Alligator Trapper," Florida Fish and Wildlife Conservation Commission, https://myfwc.com/wildlifehabitats/wildlife/alligator/snap/how-to-be-a-nat/.

Trappers could make: Tim Williams interview.

"How to Skin": deermeatfordinner, "How to Skin, De-bone and Flesh out an Alligator," April 16, 2013, YouTube video, 22.53, https://www.youtube.com/watch?v=exv6JomUk5A&t=212s.

"Butcher a Massive Alligator": deermeatfordinner, "{GRAPHIC} How to Butcher a Massive Alligator," August 30, 2016, YouTube video, 14.12, https://www.youtube.com/watch?v=FLaXcxE5spI&t=1s.

"Clean, Fillet, Debone": FLSportsman, "How to Clean, Fillet, Debone and Skin an Alligator," August 16, 2013, YouTube, video, 10.59, https://www.youtube.com/watch?v=o7iiV3CMo5I.

An 8-inch head: These prices taken from Worldwide Wildlife Products in October 2019. "Alligator Heads, Gator Heads," Worldwide Wildlife Products, https://www.worldwidewildlifeproducts.com/store/pc/Alligator-Heads-Gator-Heads-c28.htm.

small souvenirs could be made: Robert McDade, CEO of Natural Selections, qtd. by Leigh Buchanan in "Need an Alligator Head? This Guy Can Hook You Up," *Inc. Magazine*, March 10, 2015, https://www.inc.com/leigh-buchanan/need-an-alligator-head-this-guy-can-hook-you-up.html.

could make a lot of money: Dialogue from Paul Bedard's show at Everglades Holiday Park in February 2017.

Native Americans lived: Dept. of Anthropology & Genealogy Seminole Tribe of Florida, https://www.semtribe.com/STOF.

These battles: Ibid.

"We once had twelve clans": Billy Walker, interview by the author, February 2019, recorded by Sofia Valiente in Hollywood, FL. Valiente took photos for the article I wrote for *VICE*, and she recorded an interview with Walker before I met up with them at the Pow Wow.

The remaining eight clans: "Clans," Seminole Tribe of Florida online, https://www.semtribe.comSTOF/culture/clans.

"There used to be an alligator clan": Billy Walker interview.

In the early 1900s, some: "A Timeline for Survival: 500 Years of Seminole History," Dept. of Anthropology & Genealogy Seminole Tribe of Florida, https://www.semtribe.com/STOF/history/timeline.

"You're a bad boy": Dialogue from Billy Walker's performance in February 2019 in Hollywood, Florida.

the Floridian had swum: Mary Thorn, interview by the author, May 2019.

The Great Malenko: Ibid.

Mary's job at the gator show: Ibid.

people could keep an American alligator: "Alligator Permits: Alligators in Captivity," Florida Fish and Wildlife Conservation Commission, https:// myfwc.com/license/wildlife/alligator-permits/.

"There's a lot of people": Mary Thorn interview.

License applicants: "Alligator Permits: Alligators in Captivity," Florida Fish and Wildlife Conservation Commission, https://myfwc.com/license/wildlife/ alligator-permits/.

"Perhaps, they would": Laura Brandt, correspondence with the author, October 2019.

She did not live: Monivette Cordeiro, "Lakeland Woman Fights to Keep Rambo, Her 6-Foot-Long Pet Alligator," *Orlando Weekly*, March 17, 2016, https://www.orlandoweekly.com/Blogs/archives/2016/03/17/ lakeland-woman-fights-to-keep-rambo-her-6-foot-long-pet-alligator.

"Florida Woman Fights to Keep": Avianne Tan, "Florida Woman Fights to Keep Her Pet Alligator Who Wears Clothes and 'Rides' ATVs," ABC News, March 17, 2016, https://abcnews.go.com/US/ florida-woman-fights-pet-alligator-wears-clothesrides/story?id=37717980.

A lawyer: Thorn said the lawyer wanted to remain anonymous.

For her to keep Rambo: Mary Thorn interview.

"He won't bite you": Tim Williams interview.

Owen Godwin Sr. opened: "Historical Timeline," Gatorland, https://www. gatorland.com/about/about-gatorland/gatorland-historical-time-line/.

Owen bought 16 acres: Ibid.

He originally named the park: Dorothy Mays, "Gatorland: Survival of the Fittest among Florida's Mid-tier Tourist Attractions" (2009), *Faculty Publications*, 151, http://scholarship.rollins.edu/asfacpub/151/.

a record-setting 75 million tourists: "Orlando Announces Record 75 Million Visitors," Visit Orlando, https://www.visitorlando.com/en/corporate-blog/ post/orlando-announces-record-75-million-visitors.

Gatorland survived: Tim Williams interview.

"notoriously cruel alligator park": "Alligator and Turtle Displays Are Removed from Two Florida McDonald's," People for the Ethical Treatment of Animals (PETA), April 2002, https://www.peta.org/about-peta/victories/ alligator-turtle-displays-removed-two-florida-mcdonalds/.

"Right now, the white ibis": Diane Brannon, interview by the author, February 2017.

"Crocodile! Croc, Sultan": Tim Williams interview.

Researchers estimated anywhere: Michael Dorcas qtd. in Kevin Dennehy, "Tracking the Big Snakes Devouring the Everglades," *Yale Environment 360*, Yale School of Forestry & Environmental Studies, September 12, 2012.

The snakes had altered: Michael Dorcas qtd. in Kevin Dennehy, ibid.

This area had once covered: Lance Gunderson, Stephen S. Light, and C. S. Holling, "Lessons from the Everglades," *BioScience* 45 (1995): S66–S73, https://www.jstor.org/stable/1312447?seq=1#page_scan_tab_contents.

"one boundless expanse": "Notes on the Passage across the Everglades," *The News* (St. Augustine), January 8, 1841: *Tequesta*, no. 20 (1960): 57–65, http://digitalcollections.fiu.edu/tequesta/files/1960/60_1_06.pdf.

"an impenetrable barrier": Alonzo Church, "A Dash through the Everglades," *Tequesta*, no. 9 (1949): 13–42, http://digitalcollections.fiu.edu/tequesta/files/1949/49_1_02.pdf.

"wild turkey, broiled and fried curlew": George Henry Preble, "A Canoe Expedition into the Everglades in 1842," *Tequesta*, no. 5 (1945): 30–51.

"wild beasts, reptiles, and strange birds": Chas. H. Pratt, "Everglades Explored: The Only Successful Attempt on Record," *Tropical Sun*, August 19, 1891, https://ufdc.ufl.edu/UF00075915/00447/2x.

"could walk across their heads": Alonzo Church, "A Dash through the Everglades," *Tequesta*, no. 9 (1949): 13–42, http://digitalcollections.fiu.edu/tequesta/files/1949/49_1_02.pdf.

"a thousand other horrors": Ibid.

"large as a goose": Chas. H. Pratt, "Everglades Explored: The Only Successful Attempt on Record," *Tropical Sun*, August 19, 1891, https://ufdc.ufl.edu/UF00075915/00447/2x.

"The snakes in front of us": Church, "A Dash through the Everglades," 13–42, http://digitalcollections.fiu.edu/tequesta/files/1949/49_1_02.pdf.

"struck by rattlesnakes": Pratt, "Everglades Explored," https://ufdc.ufl.edu/UF00075915/00447/2x.

"soon got used to": Ibid.

the longest Burmese python ever caught: "Invasive Burmese Python," FWC, https://myfwc.com/wildlifehabitats/profiles/reptiles/snakes/burmese-python/.

region encompassed 1.5 million acres: "Everglades," National Park Service, https://www.nps.gov/ever/planyourvisit/index.htm.

He preferred to grab pythons: Leo Sanchez, interview by the author, January 2016.

culturally associated with death: Jacob Olesen, "Fear of Snakes Phobia–Ophidiophobia," FearOf.net, https://www.fearof.net/fear-of-snakes-phobia-ophidiophobia/.

Polls showed: Fear of snakes: 2001 Gallup poll, 50 percent, Rick Blizzard, "Preventative Care: The Fear Factor," Gallup, April 9, 2002, https://news.gallup.com/poll/5761/Preventative-Care-Fear-Factor.aspx. Fear of snakes: 2018 Chapman University Survey of American Fears, 24.1 percent, https://

www.chapman.edu/wilkinson/research-centers/babbie-center/_files/fear-2018/Complete-Fears-2018-ranked.pdf.

"core mammalian heritage": Arne Öhman and Susan Mineka, "The Malicious Serpent: Snakes as a Prototypical Stimulus for an Evolved Module of Fear," *Current Directions in Psychological Science* 12, no. 1 (2003): 5–9, http://www.jstor.org.umiss.idm.oclc.org/stable/20182821.

Miami's port turned south Florida: K. Smith et al., "Summarizing US Wildlife Trade with an Eye toward Assessing the Risk of Infectious Disease Introduction," *EcoHealth* 14, no. 1 (2017): 29–39, https://link.springer.com/article/10.1007/s10393-017-1211-7.

Between 1996 and 2006: U.S. Fish and Wildlife Service as cited in "To Amend Title 18, United States Code, to Prohibit the Importation of Various Injurious Species of Constrictor Snakes," *U.S. House Journal*, September 28, 2012, https://www.govinfo.gov/content/pkg/CRPT-112hrpt691/pdf/CRPT-112hrpt691-pt1.pdf.

The International Union for Conservation: "Burmese Python" listed as "vulnerable" as of August 9, 2020, https://www.iucnredlist.org/species/193451/2237271.

Convention on International Trade: Rosalind Reeve, *Policing International Trade in Endangered Species: The CITES Treaty and Compliance*. Abingdon: Routledge, 2014.

In 2010, the State of Florida: Steve Johnson, "The Invader Updater—Legislation," University of Florida, Dept. of Wildlife Ecology and Conservation, http://ufwildlife.ifas.ufl.edu/invader updater/legislation.shtml.

The first reported: "Nonnative Snakes," Florida Fish and Wildlife Conservation Commission, https://myfwc.com/wildlifehabitats/nonnatives/reptiles/snakes/.

Along with pythons: Ibid.

Some non-native species: "Florida's Nonnative Fish and Wildlife," FWC, https://myfwc.com/wildlifehabitats/nonnatives/.

The hurricane destroyed: Michael L. Avery, Richard Engeman, Kandy Keacher, John Humphrey, William Bruce, Tom Mathies, and Richard E. Mauldin, "Cold Weather and the Potential Range of Invasive Burmese Pythons," *Biological Invasions* 12, no. 11 (2010): 3649–52, https://link.springer.com/article/10.1007/s10530-010-9761-4.

"240 pounds of python": Ian Bartoszek qtd. in Kate Baggaley, "Pythons Are Invading Florida: Meet the Scientists Fighting Back," *Popular Science* online, October 13, 2017, https://www.popsci.com/florida-invasive-pythons/.

Cypress, pine hummocks, and palmetto scrub: George Henry Preble, "A Canoe Expedition into the Everglades in 1842," *Tequesta*, no. 5 (1945): 30–51.

opened his first pizza place: Evan Daniell, interview by the author, January 2015.

People couldn't eat: Ibid.

"People are pretty nervous": Emma Daniell, interview by the author, January 2015.

"If you watch shows": Jenny Novak, interview by the author, January 2016.

These snakes got caught: Ian Bartoszek qtd. in Baggaley, "Pythons Are Invading Florida," https://www.popsci.com/florida-invasive-pythons/.

"I've always loved snakes": Brandon Robbins interview.

If a person reached in front: Jenny Novak interview.

the first Great Python Challenge: Croc Docs, "2013 Python Challenge Evaluation and Attitude Survey," University of Florida, http://crocdoc.ifas.ufl.edu/projects/pythonchallenge2013/.

participated in the inaugural hunt: Leo Sanchez interview.

He worked with alligators, iguanas: Brian Wood, interview by the author, January 2016.

The native Floridian: Tim Meyer, interview by the author, January 2016.

His wife told a newspaper: Douglas Martin, "Bill Haast, a Man Charmed by Snakes, Dies at 100," *New York Times*, June 17, 2011, https://www.nytimes.com/2011/06/18/us/18haast.html.

"who took it to a whole": Tim Meyer interview.

like an Everglades version: Joseph Stromber, "On the Trail of Florida's Bigfoot—the Skunk Ape," *Smithsonian Magazine*, March 6, 2014, https://www.smithsonianmag.com/science-nature/trail-floridas-bigfoot-skunk-ape-180949981/.

"great way to decompress": Tom Aycock, interview by the author, January 2016.

"This is my happy place": Leo Sanchez interview.

"Did you have any luck": Haley Hanson, interview by the author, January 2016.

"I pulled it out and grabbed": Matt Briggle, interview by the author, January 2016.

REPTILE PEOPLE

A pet smuggler: Name withheld for anonymity.

He started smuggling in the 1970s: Tom Crutchfield, interview by the author, April 2018.

"a genetic predisposition to love": Ibid.

"With the anaconda securing": "Ross Allen Reptile Institute (1960s)," Florida Memory, State Archives of Florida, 1.29, https://www.floridamemory.com/items/show/232386.

"raw material for antivenom": Bryan Christy, *The Lizard King: The True Crimes and Passions of the World's Greatest Reptile Smugglers* (New York: Hachette, 2008).

"a lot, a lot, a lot": Tom Crutchfield interview.

He sold to private: Ibid.

At his peak in the mid-eighties: Ibid.

In 1995, Tom was convicted: "Reptile Dealer Sentenced for Conspiracy, Wildlife Smuggling," U.S. Fish & Wildlife Service, Division of Public Affairs, April 22, 2000, https://www.fws.gov/news/ShowNews.cfm?ID=A11C3CD1-AC20-11D4-A179009027B6B5D3.

During this same time: Ibid.

Operation Chameleon found: Ibid.

Tom had concealed the reptiles: "U.S. Reptile Dealer Faces Wildlife Smuggling and Conspiracy Charge," U.S. Fish and Wildlife Service, August 7, 1998, https://www.fws.gov/news/Historic/NewsReleases/1998/19980807b.pdf.

In 2000, a court: "Reptile Dealer Sentenced for Conspiracy, Wildlife Smuggling," U.S. Fish & Wildlife Service, Division of Public Affairs, April 22, 2000, https://www.fws.gov/news/ShowNews. cfm?ID=A11C3CD1-AC20–11D4-A179009027B6B5D3.

The court sentenced him: "Reptile Smuggler Sentenced for Trafficking in Rare Species," U.S. Department of Justice, April 16, 1999, https://www.justice. gov/archive/opa/pr/1999/April/140enr.htm.

"import, export, sell": "Lacey Act," U.S. Fish & Wildlife Service International Affairs, https://www.fws.gov/international/laws-treaties-agreements/us-conservation-laws/lacey-act.html.

She'd brought the long-legged rodent: Susan Barr, interview by the author, June 2019.

She liked seeing the variety: Emma Dixon, interview by the author, June 2019.

"It's big": Arne Haryn, interview by the author, June 2019.

in 2014, Robert was sentenced: "Two Florida Reptile Dealers Sentenced to Prison for Conspiring and Trafficking in Protected Reptiles," U.S. Department of Justice, December 8, 2014, https://www.justice.gov/opa/pr/ two-florida-reptile-dealers-sentenced-prison-conspiring-and-trafficking-protected-reptiles.

Arne had spent the latter part: Arne Haryn interview.

provide two letters of reference: from "Florida Fish and Wildlife Conservation Commission Application for VRC—License to Possess or Exhibit Venomous Reptiles and/or Reptiles of Concern," https://myfwc.com/media/16367/ permits_venrepapp0809.pdf.

"more blackwater events happening": Scott Wisneski, interview by the author, June 2019.

"proactively protect Florida": "New FWC Nonnative Species Rules Take Effect May 2," FWC, https://myfwc.com/news/all-news/nonnative-rules/.

She'd met Crutchfield through Facebook: Stacey Maltz, interview by the author, April 2018.

"A cat is fuzzy, soft, cute": Rod Sadler, interview by the author, April 2018.

One Floridian reportedly picked up: Ron Magill on *All Things Considered*, "What to Do If You Come across a Frozen Iguana," NPR, January 5, 2018, https://www.npr.org/2018/01/05/576082463/ what-to-do-if-you-come-across-a-frozen-iguana.

Iguanas became such a big issue: "Green Iguana," FWC, https://myfwc.com/ wildlifehabitats/profiles/reptiles/green-iguana/?redirect=wildlifehabitats+n onnatives+reptiles+iguanas-and-relatives+green-iguana.

"People don't like the feral iguanas": Tom Crutchfield interview.

"has placed reptiles at Tom Crutchfield's facility": Carol Lyn Parrish, FWC

South (West Palm Beach), personal communication with the author, October 2019.

"I don't like to see": Tom Crutchfield interview.

he coauthored an article: William Hayes, Samuel Cyril, Tom Crutchfield, Joseph Wasilewski, Thomas Rothfus, and Ronald Carter, "Conservation of the Endangered San Salvador Rock Iguanas (Cyclura rileyi rileyi): Population Estimation, Invasive Species Control, Translocation, and Headstarting," *Herpetological Conservation and Biology* 11 (2016): 90–105.

A Revelation

in the late 1920s: Brandon Haught, "'Florida Citizens for Science': Championing Florida's Science Education," *Florida Scientist* 77, no. 4 (2014): 230–35.

Florida, again, nearly passed legislation in 2008: Ibid.

The park eventually attracted visitors: Ken Storey, "In a Major Overhaul, Orlando's Holy Land Experience Will End All Theatrical Productions," *Orlando Weekly*, January 7, 2020, https://www.orlandoweekly.com/Blogs/archives/2020/01/07/in-a-major-overhaul-orlandos-holy-land-experience-will-end-all-theatrical-productions.

"everything is coated in gold": Sarah Jane W., review of The Holy Land Experience, *Yelp*, March 19, 2015, https://www.yelp.com/biz/the-holy-land-experience-orlando?start=60.

"a 75-minute orgy of blood": Ibid.

Ybor City, once known: Elizabeth Rodriguez Fielder, "Designing Latinidad: Gulf South Migration and Contemporary Gentrification in Ybor City, Florida," *Global South* 12, no. 1 (2018): 89–111.

In 2017, the City of Tampa passed: Vazzo v. City of Tampa, No. 8:17-cv-2896-T-02AAS, 2–3 (M.D. Fla. Oct. 4, 2019), https://casetext.com/case/vazzo-v-city-of-tampa.

listed the ethical issues: Jack Drescher, Alan Schwartz, Flávio Casoy, Christopher A. McIntosh, Brian Hurley, Kenneth Ashley, Mary Barber et al., "The Growing Regulation of Conversion Therapy," *Journal of Medical Regulation* 102, no. 2 (2016): 7–12, https://www.jmronline.org/doi/full/10.30770/2572-1852-102.2.7.

"chose to believe the truth": Alan Chambers, "I Once Led an Ex-Gay Ministry: Here's Why I Now Support People in Gay Marriages," *Washington Post*, June 26, 2015, https://www.washingtonpost.com/news/acts-of-faith/wp/2015/06/26/i-once-led-an-ex-gay-ministry-heres-why-i-now-support-people-in-gay-marriages/.

"overwhelming research": Vazzo v. City of Tampa, No. 8:17-cv-2896-T-02AAS, 2–3 (M.D. Fla. Oct. 4, 2019), https://casetext.com/case/vazzo-v-city-of-tampa.

"identify with their masculinity": RuthInstitute, "Florida Is Sued over Reparative Therapy? Robert Vazzo on Dr. J," YouTube video, 1:00:10, November 8, 2019, https://www.youtube.com/watch?v=QJ3rdk268vE.

he'd come out to Ybor to preach: Carl Junstron, interview by the author, March 2017.

"wicked thing": Dan, interview by the author, March 2017.

about six or eight people: Aaron Muñoz, interview by the author, April 2017.

The couple hadn't before seen: Dayna Lazarus, interview by the author, April 2017.

The weekly protest provided: Sarah Zaharako, interview by the author, April 2017.

A defrocked gay minister: Melissa M. Wilcox, "Of Markets and Missions: The Early History of the Universal Fellowship of Metropolitan Community Churches," *Religion and American Culture* 11, no. 1 (2001): 83–108.

"liberal evangelical": Ibid.

In 2020, MCC counted nearly: "History of MCC," Metropolitan Community Churches, https://www.mccchurch.org/overview/history-of-mcc/.

Florida has the most MCCs: "United States Church Listing, Metropolitan Churches, https://www.mccchurch.org/overview/ourchurches/find-a-church/united-states-church-listing/#9.

The Orlando church formed in 1979: Jeff Kunerth, "Generation Gap Imperils Gay Church," *Orlando Sentinel*, December 31 2010, https://www.orlandosentinel.com/news/orange-county/os-young-gays-church-future-20101231-story.html.

The Southern Baptist Convention: Glen Jeansonne, "Southern Baptist Attitudes toward Slavery, 1845–1861," *Georgia Historical Quarterly* 55, no. 4 (1971): 510–22.

"There are more and more churches": Reverend Terri Steed Pierce, interview by the author, May 2020.

Megan decided to take an internship: Megan Currie, interview by the author, May 2020.

The news made Stanley's hair: Stanley Ramos, interview by the author, May 2020.

"Orlando Massacre Brings": David Smith, "Orlando Massacre Brings together Christians and Gay Community," *The Guardian*, June 15, 2016, https://www.theguardian.com/us-news/2016/jun/15/orlando-massacre-christians-gay-community.

Reverend Terri felt otherwise: Reverend Terri Steed Pierce interview.

a lot of people still couldn't understand: Marlyn Moir, interview by the author, May 2020.

a widening gap in church attendance: Pew Research Center, "In U.S., Decline of Christianity Continues at Rapid Pace," October 17, 2019, https://www.pewforum.org/2019/10/17/in-u-s-decline-of-christianity-continues-at-rapid-pace/.

The thirty-three-year-old grew up in Wisconsin: Brian Wood, interview by the author, May 2020.

Preaching to an empty room: Reverend Terri Steed Pierce interview.

Tyler Gillespie is a poet and award-winning journalist who has written for *Rolling Stone*, *The Guardian*, *GQ*, *Salon*, *Playboy*, and elsewhere. He's the author of *Florida Man: Poems*.